The Harmonic Organization of *The Rite of Spring*

The Harmonic Organization
of
The Rite of Spring

Allen Forte

New Haven and London
Yale University Press 1978

Published with assistance from the Louis Stern Memorial Fund.

Designed by Thos. Whitridge
and set in IBM Pyramid type.
Printed in the United States of America by
The Murray Printing Co., Westford, Mass.

Published in Great Britain, Europe, Africa, and Asia (except Japan) by Yale University Press, Ltd., London. Distributed in Latin America by Kaiman & Polon, Inc., New York City; in Australia and New Zealand by Book & Film Services, Artarmon, N.S.W., Australia; and in Japan by Harper & Row, Publishers, Tokyo Office.

The firm of Boosey & Hawkes has graciously allowed the musical excerpts from *The Rite of Spring* to be produced in this volume:
The Rite of Spring
Copyright 1921 by Edition Russe de Musique
Copyright assigned 1947 to Boosey & Hawkes for all countries of the world
The Rite of Spring (Le Sacre du Printemps) Sketches
Copyright 1969 by Boosey & Hawkes Music Publishers Ltd.
Reprinted by permission of Boosey & Hawkes, Inc.

Library of Congress Cataloging in Publication Data

Forte, Allen.
  The harmonic organization of The rite of spring.

  1. Stravinskiĭ, Igor' Fedorovich, 1882–1971. Le sacre du printemps. 2. Stravinskiĭ, Igor' Fedorovich, 1882–1971—Harmonic system. I. Title.
MT100.S968F7   782.9'5'54   77-90946
ISBN 0-300-02201-8

Contents

Acknowledgments

I wish to express my gratitude to Janet Schmalfeldt for her careful reading of the manuscript and for many valuable suggestions. Alan Chapman also deserves thanks for his thoughtful reading. Residual errors, particularly those of a substantive nature, are to be attributed only to the author.

Carl A. Rosenthal autographed the musical examples in his characteristically meticulous and elegant manner. I thank him for his assistance in preparing these illustrations, which are fundamental to the study of *The Rite of Spring* presented here.

Introduction

Although Igor Stravinsky's ballet *The Rite of Spring* (1912) is universally regarded as one of the monuments of modern music, no effort has yet been made to comprehend the extraordinary way in which the pitch materials of this large-scale musical work are organized. The present study represents such an effort.

This introduction is intended to prepare the reader to understand certain technical aspects of the analysis that constitutes the main body of the study. Essentially it entails consideration of general features of pitch and interval structures and of the ways in which those structures may be interrelated to form complex and coherent musical spans.

The analytical approach to this study is fully set forth in a recent publication by the author: *The Structure of Atonal Music* (Yale University Press, New Haven and London, 2d printing, 1977).* The reader is referred to that work for more detailed discussion of certain of the structural materials and relations presented below.

Pitch Class

The notion of pitch class (pc) is implicit in ordinary musical language whenever we speak of the 12 notes of the chromatic scale. That is, it is assumed that only 12 different pitches comprise the basic stock of the chromatic system. More precisely, this means that the 12 notes can be represented in a single octave (by assuming octave equivalence) and that a particular notation for a pitch is not unique (by assuming enharmonic equivalence).

*Hereafter cited as *StrAM*

Ex. A. Reduction to pitch classes

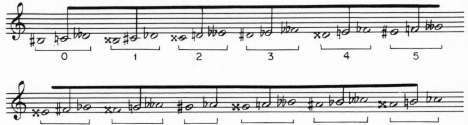

Example A illustrates: The beam connects stems of noteheads that represent the complete chromatic scale within a single octave; each of the stemmed noteheads, with the exception of Ab, has two alternative and enharmonically equivalent notations. Brackets below Ex. A group the equivalently notated pitches, and to each group is assigned a number that represents the pitch class. By convention, all three notations for the pitch C (B#, C natural, and Dbb) reduce to pitch class 0, all three notations for the pitch C# (B×, C#, Db) reduce to pitch class 1, and so on. For convenience, the designation p*ci* will often be used, where *i* is one of the integers from 0–11. The integers 0–11 are called pitch-class integers. Thus, when pc8 is mentioned, it might be notated as G# or Ab in its musical context. It should be evident that the notion of pitch class excludes information concerning register, timbre, durational value, mode of attack, and other features.

Pitch-Class Set

Given a notated collection of pitches, such as that shown in Ex. B, it is not difficult to write the corresponding pitch-class integers, separated by commas.

Ex. B. Pitch-class set notation

[2,3,6,8]

These integers, enclosed in brackets, then represent a pitch-class set, one of the 220 possible pitch-class sets within the 12 pitch-class universe. Observe that the pc integers are given in ascending order in Ex. B and that that order does not correspond to the bottom-to-top or top-to-bottom arrangement of the noteheads on the staff. In the present study pitch-class sets are always given in normal order, the order that groups the integers within the smallest distance from left to right and with the smallest successive intervals on the left. Example C shows the equivalent in ordinary notation of the pitch-class set with set listing [2,3,6,8].

Ex. C. Normal order in notation and set listing

[2,3,6,8]

It is important to notice that the integer notation of the pitch-class set does not necessarily provide any information about the ordering (arrangement) of the actual musical components. Thus, conceptually, the pitch-class set is an unordered set and differs basically, for example, from the ordered 12-tone row, in which considerations of order-position are crucial.

In addition to the integers in the bracketed pitch-class set listing there is one number of special importance associated with any set: the number of elements it contains. This is called the cardinal number and is designated by #i, where i is a number from 1 through 12. This study is mainly concerned with pitch-class sets of cardinal numbers 3–9 (#3–#9).

Pitch-Class Set Name

As indicated, above, there is a finite number of pitch-class sets, namely, 220. Each of these pitch-class sets has been assigned a name consisting of the cardinal number of the set followed by a hyphen followed by a number that gives the position of the set on a list of sets, the ordinal number. This list of sets is given as the Appendix to the present study.[†]

The set name may also include the character *Z*, which indicates that the set so designated has a counterpart of a particular nature. For example, the pitch-class set exhibited in Exx. A and B bears the name 4-Z15. This name indicates that the set contains 4 elements, that it is item 15 on the list of 4-element pitch-class sets, and that it bears a close relationship to a counterpart set (4-Z29), a relation that will be explained below.

[†]Excluded from the list are the 1-element sets, the 2-element sets, the 10-element sets, the 11-element set, and the 12-element set.

Interval Class and Interval Content

The interval between two notated pitches is measured by counting the number of half steps that separate them. Example D illustrates.

Ex. D. Interval class 4

4   8

The distance (interval) from C up to E is 4 half steps; the distance from C down to E is 8 half steps. As in ordinary musical usage, the two intervals are regarded as equivalent (by tonal inversion). Thus, corresponding to the notion of pitch class (pc), the notion of interval class (ic) can be developed. Specifically, the interval between any two notated pitches as represented by pitch-class integers can be reduced to one of the interval classes represented by the integers 1–6. This is shown in Ex. E.

Ex. E. Interval classes

In considering the intervals formed by a pitch-class set, one often wishes to take into account the total interval content, not merely the intervals formed, say, by adjacent components of the set. This can be ascertained by determining the interval class formed by every pair of elements. For set 4-Z15, formation of the total interval content is demonstrated in Ex. F: ic1 is formed by D and Eb, ic4 by D and F#, ic6 by D and Ab, and so on.

Ex. F. Total interval content of 4-Z15

Pc set 4-Z15 always has a total interval content consisting of one interval of each class. For this reason it is often called the all-interval tetrachord.

There are only two tetrachords that have this special characteristic, 4-Z15 and 4-Z29. The purpose of the letter *Z* in the set name can now be revealed: it indicates that there is a pair of sets with the same total interval content.

The total interval content of a pc set is represented by the interval vector, an ordered numerical array that displays the number of intervals of each class. The first (leftmost) number in the array gives the number of intervals of class 1, the second number gives the number of intervals of class 2, the third the number of intervals of class 3, and so on. Thus, the interval vector for both 4-Z15 and 4-Z29, the all-interval tetrachords, is [111111]. The interval vector is always enclosed in square brackets.

Transpositionally Equivalent Sets

Example G shows two sets, labeled A and B. Set B is derived by transposition from set A, and the two sets are regarded as transpositionally equivalent: Both represent pitch-class set 4-Z15.

Ex. G. Transpositionally equivalent sets (ordered)

A [2,3,6,8]   B [5,6,9,11]

Notice that the transposition in Ex. G is ordered: The first element of set B is three half steps higher than the first element of set A, the second element of set B is three half steps higher than the second element of set A, and so on. Most often in the present study, however, unordered transpositions will be of greatest importance. An instance is shown in Ex. H.

Ex. H. Transpositionally equivalent sets (unordered)

A [2,3,6,8]   B [5,6,9,11]

There set B is a transposition of set A, but there is no one-to-one correspondence with respect to the registral arrangement of the components of the two sets.

Transposition is defined for pitch-class sets in terms of the operation of addition. If the same number is added to all the integers of a pitch-class set, this effectively causes the set to be transposed. The general designation for that number is *t,* called the transposition operator. In order to describe a particular transposition it is only necessary to indicate the value of *t.* In Exx. G and H the value of *t* is 3 (or *t* = 3). The arithmetic is uncompli-cated: Add 3 to each element of set A to produce set B, thus:

$$\begin{array}{r} \text{A:} \quad 2 \quad 3 \quad 6 \quad 8 \\ +3 \qquad\qquad\qquad\qquad \\ \text{B:} \quad 5 \quad 6 \quad 9 \quad 11 \end{array}$$

Notice that if the value of *t* is 12, the result of transposition is the same as if *t* = 0.‡ Thus, there are only 12 values for *t*: the integers 0–11.

Inversionally Equivalent Sets

Example I shows two forms of pc set 4-Z15, labeled A and B.

Ex. I. Contour inversion about an initial note

Set B is an inversion of set A beginning from the same note, Eb. This is inversion in the traditional contour sense: Each successive linear interval in set A is matched by a linear interval of the same size but in the opposite direction in set B.

Example J also displays two inversionally equivalent sets—equivalent because one can be derived from the other by inversion.

Ex. J. Inversion by fixed pc correspondence

A[2, 3, 6, 8]   B[4, 6, 9, 10]   C[5, 7, 10, 11]

‡In general, the reduction of values for the transposition operator is carried out modulo 12. That is, for any integer greater than or equal to 12, compute the remainder of that number divided by 12. The same arithmetic is applied in addition. For example, 12 + 12 = 0 modulo 12.

The two sets in this instance, however, are not inverted about an axis pitch, as in Ex. I but are inverted according to a fixed correspondence between any two pitch-class integers that sum to 12 (12 = 0 modulo 12), according to this table:

0	1	2	3	4	5	6
0	11	10	9	8	7	6

The pairs of numbers in the table are said to be *inverse related*. Specifically, 0 is its own inverse, 11 is the inverse of 1, 2 is the inverse of 10, and so on. Thus for Ex. J the pc integers of set B correspond to those of set A as follows:

$$\text{A:} \quad 2 \quad 3 \quad 6 \quad 8$$
$$\text{B:} \quad 10 \quad 9 \quad 6 \quad 4$$

More precisely, set B is said to be the inversion of set A transposed, with $t = 0$. Set C in Ex. J is the inversion of set A transposed, with $t = 1$. This can easily be seen by comparing the set listing for set B with that for set C: Each integer in set B is increased by 1 in the listing for set C.

The method employed in this book is the computation of inversion beginning with the fixed correspondences shown in the table above as inversion followed by transposition for $t = 0$.

One additional aspect of Ex. J requires comment. Set B is an ordered inversion of set A: The successive vertical intervals of set A read from bottom to top as ic3, ic2, and ic6, whereas in set B the intervals are the same but in the opposite direction. In general, little attention will be paid to ordered inversions in the present study since *The Rite of Spring* does not exhibit them except in a very few instances.

Prime Form

The set listings that appear in the numbered examples of this book are always given in normal order, as indicated above. There is, however, one basic form associated with each pitch-class set type, and this basic form is called the prime form. The complete list of prime forms is given in the appendix, as has been indicated. The reader can easily verify that the particular set has been correctly identified—that is, that it reduces to the prime form corresponding to the set name on the list—by transposing the pc integers so that the listing begins with pc0 and then, if necessary, by inverting and transposing to level 0 again. We can illustrate this using the A and C forms of 4-Z15 in Ex. J:

Given A: [2,3,6,8]

Subtract first integer from each: [0,1,4,6]

Find 0,1,4,6 on set list. This is the prime form of 4-Z15.

Given C: [5,7,10,11]

Subtract first integer from each: [0,2,5,6]

Because this is not on the set list, it must be an inversion of the prime form; therefore:

Invert the set: [0,10,7,6]

Place in ascending order: [6,7,10,0]

Reduce to level 0 by subtracting first integer
    from each: [0,1,4,6]

Find 0,1,4,6 on set list. This is the prime form of 4-Z15.

Observe that in performing the subtraction to reduce to level 0, if the integer from which the first integer is being subtracted is less than the first digit, one need only add the inverse of the integer. For example, reduce [8,9,0,2] to begin with 0:

$$8 \quad 9 \quad 0 \quad 2$$
$$0 \quad 1 \quad 4 \quad 6$$

Since both 0 and 2 are less than 8, 4 (the inverse of 8) is added to those two integers.

The Inclusion Relation (Subsets and Supersets)

This relation is one of the most interesting and significant in *The Rite of Spring*. Again, it can be illustrated using 4-Z15. We already know that the set includes or contains four single-element units, namely, the pc integers. Another way to say this is that 4-Z15 contains four subsets of one element each. In Ex. K they are pc6, pc2, pc8, and pc3.

Ex. K. Three-element subsets of 4-Z15

4-Z 15: [2,3,6,8]   3-8   3-7   3-3   3-5

We also know that 4-Z15 contains six 2-element subsets, namely, the pairs of pc's that form the intervals of the set: [6,2], [6,8], [6,3], [2,8], [2,3], and [8,3]. The 3-element subsets, or trichords, of 4-Z15 are shown in Ex. K. These are of four types: 3-3, 3-5, 3-7, and 3-8. Any set of cardinal number 4 will always contain 4 subsets of cardinal number 3; however, these subsets may not always be of different types. That is, a set type may be multiply represented within a particular set. Example L illustrates.

Ex. L. Three-element subsets of 4-8

4-8: [2, 3, 7, 8]   3-4   3-5   3-5   3-4

There the four 3-element subsets of 4-8 reduce to only two types, 3-4 and 3-5. The reader can verify for himself that each pair of the same type is inversionally related.

   The subsets of 4-Z15 have now been discussed. Of course, 4-Z15 itself is a subset of a number of larger sets. For example, it is contained within 5-32, as shown in Ex. M. Here 5-32 is said to be a superset of 4-Z15.

Ex. M. Pc set 4-Z15 as a subset of 5-32

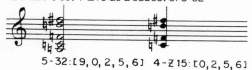

5-32: [9, 0, 2, 5, 6]   4-Z 15: [0, 2, 5, 6]

Invariance

   The two principal transformations defined for pc sets are transposition and inversion, which were discussed above. Under these transformations some pc sets may hold certain pitch classes fixed, while other pitch classes will change. This phenomenon is called invariance. Example N illustrates, using a pc set that will be encountered many times in the main body of this study: 7-31.

Ex. N. Invariance

7-31: [8,9,11,0,2,3,5]   7-31: [2,3, 5, 6, 8, 9, 11]

The form of 7-31 labeled B is a transposition of A, with $t = 6$ (an unordered transposition). As a result of applying this value of $t,$ six pitch
classes are held fixed between the two sets, namely, 8,9,11,2,3,5, forming
the hexachord 6-30. In general, whenever 7-31 is transposed, with $t = 6$,
the set 6-30 will be held fixed as an invariant hexachord. Similarly, when
7-31 is transposed, with $t = 3$, the hexachordal subset 6-27 will be held
invariant. And, remarkably, when it is transposed, with $t = 9,$ the same
subset type, 6-27, will be held invariant—not the same pitch classes, however. Since 3 and 9 are inverse related, the reader might assume that inverse-
related values of t will always result in the same invariant subset type when
the set is transposed, and, indeed, this is true.

  An invariant subset may also be created by inverting a pc set.

Ex. O. Creation of an invariant subset by inversion

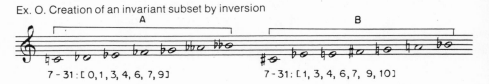

7-31: [0,1, 3, 4, 6, 7, 9]   7-31: [1, 3, 4, 6, 7, 9, 10]

In Ex. O, set B holds six of the pc's of set A fixed. The invariant subset
is 6-Z23: [1,3,4,6,7,9]. Set B is the inversion of set A transposed, with
$t = 10$.

  It is of considerable analytical interest to know what the possibilities
for invariance are, given a particular set, for one can then assess a specific
musical situation with reference to the general situation. In the case of
7-31, the greatest number of pc's that can be held invariant under transposition is 6. This will be referred to as maximum invariance for 7-31
under transposition. The least number that can be held invariant under
transposition is 3. This will be called minimum invariance for 7-31 under
transposition. Under inversion, maximum invariance for 7-31 is 6 pc's,
the same as under transposition. However, minimum invariance under
inversion is 2 pc's, which is not possible under transposition. Thus, the
choice of operations often significantly affects the invariance conditions
of a set.

The Complement Relation

In Ex. P another prominent set of *The Rite of Spring* is displayed: 7–32.

Ex. P. Complement-related sets

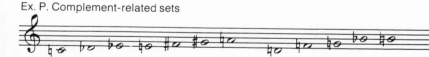

7 – 32 : [0,1, 3, 4, 6, 8, 9]   5 – 32 : [2, 5, 7, 10, 11]

The remaining five pc's not in 7–32 are also shown in the example. These form the complement of 7–32. In general, the complement of a pc set may be found by writing out the pc's not in that set. It should be pointed out that the occurrence of ordinal number 32 in the set names 7–32 and 5–32 is not accidental. Sets with the same ordinal number and with inverse-related cardinal numbers are complement related. Thus, the name of the complement of 4-Z15 is 8-Z15. (The one exception to this, the Z-hexachords, will be explained below.)

Example P is an instance of literal complementation. However, given two complement-related pc sets it should be evident that one or both of them could be transformed (transposed or inverted) without losing the fundamental association between them. Thus, the transformed complement is an extension of the literal complement, including those cases in which the pc's of the two sets may overlap.

It is even possible that the smaller member of the complement-related pair might be transformed in such a way as to be contained in the larger set. This case, called the embedded complement, is illustrated in Ex. Q: Every pc in 5–32 is also a pc in 7–32.

Ex. Q. Embedded complement

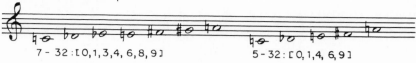

7 – 32 : [0,1, 3, 4, 6, 8, 9]   5 – 32 : [0, 1, 4, 6, 9]

Hexachords without the Z designation are self-complementary. That is, pc set 6–27, for example, is the complement of pc set 6–27. Moreover, given any form of 6–27, the complement can be derived by transposing or inverting that form. The hexachords with the Z designation, however, comprise a special and interesting case, one that is exemplified many times in *The Rite of Spring*. Each of these hexachords pairs off with another hexachord on the basis of identical interval content, which is what the Z signifies, as will be recalled. However, it is not possible to relate the two sets by transposition or by inversion, the basis for equivalency of pc sets. Accordingly, the sets are assigned unique names, and the discrepancy between the regular hexachords and the Z-hexachords is reflected in the arrangement of the set list in the appendix. Thus, no complement is listed for 6-27, for instance, whereas 6-Z13 is paired off with 6-Z42, its Z-correspondent and complement.

As a notational convenience, sets of cardinal 7 or greater may occasionally be listed using complement notation. For example, instead of listing the pc's of a 9-element set in square brackets it is possible to accurately specify the pc content of the set by listing the literal 3-element complement in rounded brackets (parentheses). For example, some form of 8-Z15, the complement of 4-Z15, might be displayed as (0,1,4,6).

Set Complexes K and Kh

A set complex is a group of sets related to a single set, called the nexus set, by the inclusion relation. There are two types of set complexes: a large, all-inclusive type called K and a more restrictive type called Kh.

Given a set A and its complement B, the set complex K consists of all the sets that are in an inclusion relation (subset or superset) with either A or B. Those sets are said to be in the set complex K *about* the pair A/B. Or, more simply, they are said to be in the set complex K about the nexus set A (or, alternatively, the nexus set B).§

Suppose one wished to determine if a particular set is in the set complex K about 5-32, say, the set 6-Z44. Now it can be ascertained that 6-Z44 is not a subset of 7-32. However, 5-32 is a subset of 6-Z44. Hence the inclusion relation holds and 6-Z44 is a member of the set complex K about 5-32/7-32.

For a set to be a member of the set complex Kh about a set A and its complement B, it must be in an inclusion relation to both A and B. For example, set 6-27 is a subset of 7-32 and also contains 5-32, and therefore qualifies for membership in the set complex Kh about 5-32/7-32.

One additional rule applies to both the set complex K and the set complex Kh: If the set complex is about sets A and B, no member of the set complex may be of the same cardinal number as A and B. For example, the set complexes K and Kh about 5-32 exclude sets of cardinal numbers 5 and 7. This does not mean that consideration of inclusion relations between sets of cardinal numbers 5 and 7 is ruled out in analysis, of course,

§In general, this is symbolized as K (set name), e.g., K (5-32).

but merely that sets of those sizes are excluded from the set complexes about sets of the same sizes.

Although the notion of the set complex is not applied often in the first part of the study that follows, it is mentioned several times and is basic to the summary discussion of certain fundamental structural components that bind the music together. For these reasons it may be of interest to the reader to see a complete roster of set complex members for a particular nexus set. This is provided by Ex. R for the sets 5–32 and 7–32.

Both K and Kh in Ex. R are characteristically symmetrical. This is most obvious in the case of cardinal numbers 9 and 3, 8 and 4. Thus, every 9-element set corresponds to its complement among the 3-element sets, and the same holds for the 8- and 4-element sets. The slash joining pairs of ordinal numbers (e.g., 6-Z19/44) indicates that those sets are complement related. Thus every hexachord pairs off with its complement. (Recall that non-Z-hexachords are self-complementary.)

The difference in size (number of members) between K and Kh in Ex. R is remarkable but typical.‖ Whereas the set complex K contains 76 member sets, the set complex Kh contains only 24. Because the set complex Kh is more "discriminating" it usually is of more interest in an analytical application.

Similarity Relations

Thus far several types of relations between pc sets have been presented: equivalence relations based upon transposition and inversion, inclusion and complement relations. It is also possible to define relations of similarity between pc sets of the same cardinal number based upon pitch-class similarity and upon interval-class similarity. Consider, for example, the prime forms and interval vectors of the two sets 5–16 and 5–32:¶

	Prime form	Interval vector
5–16	[0,1,3,4,7]	[213211]
5–32	[0,1,4,6,9]	[113221]

It is apparent that the interval vectors of the two sets exactly correspond with respect to four entries, the entries representing interval classes, 2, 3, 4,

‖Typical for all set complexes except those about non-Z-hexachords. Set complexes K and Kh are identical in those cases.

¶Sets of cardinal 5 are used here only for purposes of illustration. The concepts presented apply to sets of any cardinal number.

Example R
The set complex K about 5-32/7-32

Cardinal number	Ordinal number
9	2,3,4,5,6,7,8,9,10,11,12
8	3,7,8,10,11,12,13,14,Z15,16,17,18,19 20,22,23,24,26,27,28,Z29
6	Z19/44,Z24/46,Z25/47,27,Z28/49,Z29/50,31
4	3,7,8,10,11,12,13,14,Z15,16,17,18,19 20,22,23,24,26,27,28,Z29
3	2,3,4,5,6,7,8,9,10,11,12

The set complex Kh about 5-32/7-32

Cardinal number	Ordinal number
9	3,5,7,8,10,11
8	Z15,17,18,26,27
6	27,31
4	Z15,17,18,26,27
3	3,5,7,8,10,11

and 6. This correspondence of four vector entries is the greatest possible correspondence for any two vectors of sets of the same cardinal number; hence, the two sets may be regarded as *maximally similar with respect to interval class*. This relation is designated R1. Observe that the non-identical entries, for interval classes 1 and 5, exchange numbers.

If two 5-element sets are not equivalent by virtue of transposition or inversion (i.e., reducible to the same prime form by one of those operations), it is still possible that they might potentially be almost identical, that is, that they might share four pitch classes or, to say the same thing in terms of the inclusion relation, that they might share a common subset of 4 elements. Example S shows that this holds for pc sets 5-16 and 5-32: Both sets contain a subset of type 4-18.** This relation, based upon pitch class, is designated Rp.

Ex. S. The relation Rp (weakly represented)

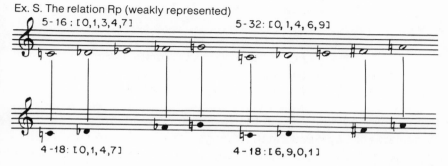

Since the two forms of 4-18 in Ex. S are not identical with respect to pitch class, the relation Rp is said to be *weakly represented*. It is, however, always possible that Rp may be *strongly represented*. Example T demonstrates: Both in 5-16 and in 5-32, 4-18 has the form [0,1,4,7].

Ex. T. The relation Rp (strongly represented)

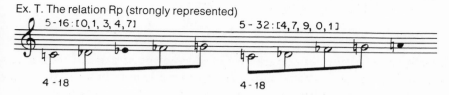

In connection with the description of the relation R1 above it was pointed out that the nonidentical entries exchange numbers: that is, that the total array of integers for both interval vectors is the same. It is also possible for two vectors of 5-element sets to have four identical entries while the nonidentical entries do not exchange:

**Sets 5-16 and 5-32 also share another 4-element set, 4-17.

	Prime form	*Interval vector*
5–Z18	[0,1,4,5,7]	[212221]
5–32	[0,1,4,6,9]	[113221]

Here the entries for interval classes 2, 4, 5 and 6 are identical in both vectors. The entries for classes 1 and 3, however, do not exchange as in the case of the vectors for 5–16 and 5–32 presented above (the relation R1). This type of intervallic similarity relation is designated R2.

Again, in the case of 5–Z18 and 5–32, the relation Rp holds as well as the relation R2. Thus, the two sets are maximally similar with respect to interval class and with respect to pitch class. This combined relation is not obligatory. Indeed, there are far more set pairs related on the basis of interval-class similarity or pitch-class similarity alone than in combination.

Finally, there is the case of *maximal dissimilarity based on interval vector*, the relation R0. Consider 5–32 and 5–35, both prominent in *The Rite of Spring*.

	Prime form	*Interval vector*
5–32	[0,1,4,6,9]	[113221]
5–35	[0,2,4,7,9]	[032140]

No two corresponding entries in the two vectors are identical.

It is remarkable, however, that although the two sets are maximally dissimilar with respect to interval content, they are maximally similar with respect to pitch class, for they share a subset of four elements. Example U illustrates.

Ex. U. The relations R0 and Rp

Usually, similarity relations are discussed in terms of pairs of sets, that is, duples. But in certain cases similarity relations extend beyond the duple to link up triples, quadruples, and so on. For example, the sets 4–12, 4–13, 4–18, and 4–27 are all interrelated by R1 and Rp. That is, *any* pair selected from this group of four will exhibit the two relations. Furthermore, they all share a common trichord, 3–10. This type of relation is called *transitive*, and there is an extraordinary example in the final movement of *The Rite of Spring*.

No attempt has been made in this introduction to show the multiple ways in which pitch-class sets and relations may be manifested in a musical work. They will vary greatly, depending upon the way in which the composer projects his musical ideas in the particular composition. Indeed, a major focus of the subsequent part of this book is upon the special and characteristic musical forms presented in *The Rite of Spring* and their interpretation in terms of pitch-class sets and relations among them.

Because the material in this introduction is general, it can be applied to the study of any possible pitch formations, not only to those that are familiar in tonal music. This is of great consequence for *The Rite of Spring.* as will become evident in the section that follows.

The Harmonic Vocabulary

In *The Rite of Spring* Stravinsky employed extensively for the first time the new harmonies that first emerged in the works of Schoenberg and Webern around 1907–08.[1] Indeed, *The Rite of Spring* is a veritable catalog of the new sonorities. Of the 50 possible hexachords, 35 are used in the work. All 38 five-note sets (and/or their seven-note complements) occur somewhere in the music, as do all but one of the four- and eight-note sets.[2]

This is not to say, however, that the sets are used in an indiscriminate way. On the contrary, there is considerable variation in prominence among sets. Some of them occur in every movement, while others are more sparsely represented. Some idea of the distribution may be gained by examining Tables 1–3, which show the occurrence of sets in the various movements. The correspondence of movements to the numbers along the top line in the tables is as follows:

1. Introduction to Part 1
2. Augurs of Spring (R13)
3. Ritual of Abduction (R37)
4. Spring Rounds (R48)
5. Ritual of Two Rival Tribes (R57)
6. Procession of the Sage (R67)
7. Kiss of the Earth (R71)
8. Dance of the Earth (R72)
9. Introduction to Part 2 (R79)
10. Mystic Circle of the Adolescents (R91)
11. Honoring of the Chosen One (R104)
12. Evocation of the Ancestors (R121)
13. Ritual of the Ancestors (R129)
14. Sacrificial Dance (R142)

1. Two shorter works of the same period (1911–13), *Le Roi des Etoiles* and the *Two Poems of Balmont,* also used the new harmonies.
2. In referring to these pitch collections the names given in the Appendix will be used, as explained in the introduction.

Table 1
Sets and Movements (Tetrachords)

	1	2	3	4	5	6	7	8	9	10	11	12	13	14
4-1	*									*				
4-2					*					*			*	*
4-3						*					*		*	
4-4										*	*			*
4-5			*		*					*	*			*
4-6	*				*						*			
4-7			*	*									*	
4-8	*	*	*	*						*	*			*
4-9						*				*	*			
4-10	*	*		*	*			*		*			*	
4-11	*	*	*	*						*			*	
4-12	*				*	*	*			*	*		*	*
4-13		*			*	*				*	*			
4-14		*							*	*	*		*	
4-Z15	*		*							*	*		*	*
4-16	*								*	*	*			*
4-17	*	*			*					*				
4-18	*		*	*	*	*				*	*	*	*	*
4-19													*	
4-20			*						*					
4-21				*		*	*	*						*
4-22		*							*					*
4-23	*	*	*											
4-25						*			*	*				
4-26		*										*		
4-27	*	*							*		*			
4-28		*				*			*	*	*			
4-Z29	*							*		*		*		

Table 2
Sets and Movements (Pentachords)

	1	2	3	4	5	6	7	8	9	10	11	12	13	14
5-1		*								*			*	
5-2	*	*												
5-3													*	
5-4	*									*	*			
5-5											*			*
5-6										*	*			*
5-7						*					*			*
5-8											*			*
5-9						*			*	*	*			
5-10		*						*					*	*
5-11				*	*						*		*	*
5-Z12		*			*								*	*
5-13			*											*
5-14					*				*		*			*
5-15										*				
5-16			*	*	*					*				*
5-Z17	*												*	*
5-Z18				*			*		*	*	*			
5-19	*					*				*				*
5-20	*										*			*
5-21		*		*					*				*	*
5-22		*		*			*							*
5-23	*	*	*							*				*
5-24							*							
5-25		*		*					*	*	*			*
5-26	*			*	*			*	*		*		*	
5-27			*						*	*				*
5-28						*			*	*	*			*
5-29	*			*						*				*
5-30				*	*									*
5-31	*	*	*	*	*	*			*	*	*		*	*
5-32	*	*	*	*					*	*		*	*	*
5-33		*												
5-34	*	*						*	*				*	*
5-35	*	*		*										
5-Z36				*	*						*			
5-Z37					*									
5-Z38				*		*			*		*		*	*

21

Table 3
Sets and Movements (Hexachords)

	1	2	3	4	5	6	7	8	9	10	11	12	13	14
6-1										*				
6-2	*	*											*	
6-Z36										*	*			
6-Z4											*			*
6-5						*							*	
6-Z6	*				*									
6-7						*					*			
6-8	*													*
6-Z10				*			*			*				*
6-Z39									*	*				*
6-Z41						*			*					
6-Z13										*			*	*
6-Z42									*					*
6-15			*	*					*				*	*
6-16									*					*
6-Z17	*			*	*				*					
6-Z43			*					*	*					*
6-Z19				*					*				*	*
6-Z44	*	*		*					*					*
6-Z23												*		*
6-Z45														*
6-Z24													*	
6-Z46	*			*					*			*		*
6-Z25									*				*	*
6-Z47				*		*								
6-27	*	*	*			*			*	*		*		*
6-Z28	*	*				*								*
6-Z49				*				*	*	*				*
6-Z29				*										*
6-Z50		*		*	*				*					*
6-30		*	*			*			*					*
6-31									*					*
6-32	*	*	*	*						*				
6-33	*			*				*	*	*				*
6-34	*					*		*		*				
6-35						*		*						*

22

(In Tables 1–3 cardinal number 5 may also refer to its inverse, 7, and the same holds for cardinal numbers 4 and 8.)

The present study considers in detail the general "harmonic" aspect of *The Rite of Spring*, by which is meant not merely the chords or verticals, but the unordered pitch-class sets (pc sets) that underlie melodic configurations, combinations of horizontal lines, and segments of various shapes. As its title indicates, this essay has as its subject the pitch structures of the work.

Tables 1–3 indicate that a number of pc sets recur throughout *The Rite of Spring*. Mention of these recurring sets is virtually non-existent in the literature, probably for two reasons. First, the sets occur in a variety of contexts, in various spacings, with varied instrumentation, and so on—in short, they are often not associated in any obvious way. (A systematic method of identifying unordered pc sets solves this problem.) Second, a small set may be represented by its larger complement (and the reverse, of course). For example, the complement-related pair 4–18 and 8–18 occurs in 10 of the 14 movements. Five occurrences are shown in Exx. 1–5.[3]

Ex. 1. *Introduction to Part 1:* R6+10

In Ex. 1 and elsewhere in the music, 4–18 or its complement 8–18 serves to delineate a formal division. Other harmonies have this articulative role as well, as will be pointed out.

---

3. The examples were derived by the author from the orchestral score published in 1921 (see n. 5), unless otherwise indicated. They are notated at concert pitch, and rehearsal numbers are designated by *R*. Examples marked *Piano Duet* are drawn from the first score of *The Rite of Spring*, prepared by Stravinsky for the ballet rehearsals and published by Edition Russe de Musique in 1913. I decided to use these two original sources in this study because there is no record available of when, why, and by whom changes were made in subsequent editions, although one can assume that Stravinsky at least approved all changes. There is, however, no reliable critical apparatus associated with this music. For a discussion of the problem of editions see Claudio Spies's fine article, "Editions of Stravinsky's Music," in Benjamin Boretz and Edward T. Cone, eds., *Perspectives on Schoenberg and Stravinsky* (New York: Norton, 1972).

Ex. 2. *Spring Rounds:* R53

The excerpt shown in Ex. 2 is from the beginning of a new section that is essentially the culmination of the quiet and repetitive music that begins the movement (R49). The crucial new component here is the subset 4-18 (bracketed in Ex. 2), a fixed feature of the passage from R53 up to R54 and the one that accounts for the skew effect, with reference to the completely diatonic section that precedes it.[4]

Ex. 3a. *Ritual of the Rival Tribes:* R58+5

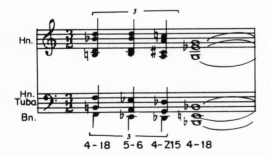

The well-known cadential passage in the *Ritual of Two Rival Tribes* at R58+5 shown in Ex. 3a ends with set 4-18, as indicated. The full score, from which the example is drawn, differs markedly both from the piano

---

4. Sketches for *The Rite of Spring* have been published in *The Rite of Spring: Sketches 1911–1913* (London: Boosey & Hawkes, 1969). See this Sketchbook, p. 7, where 4-18 is the subset in the earliest sketch for the passage but not at the same pitch level as in the final version. Thus, the subset is independent from the outset and, more important, it is evident that the set as a sonority has priority over any particular pitch-class form it might take.

duet (Ex. 3b) and from the two complete sketches in the Sketchbook (p. 25).

Ex. 3b. Piano Duet: R58+5

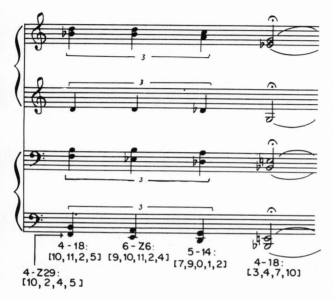

In all, there are four sketches in the Sketchbook relevant to the final version of the passage at R58+5. In the first of these, an ink sketch displayed in Ex. 3c, the first chord is 4–18, as in the duet and full score. The final chord of this sketch, although it is the same type of set as that in the final version (4–18), is a transposition of that chord, with $t = 2$ (cf. n. 4).

Ex. 3c. Sketchbook p. 25

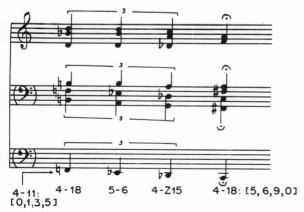

In the excerpt from the second sketch, Ex. 3d (also in ink), the composer has transposed the final chord so that it corresponds, with respect to pitch class, to the final version. However, the vertical arrangement differs; in particular, the bass note is E instead of Bb. (The preceding chords are the same as those shown in Ex. 3c.)

Ex. 3d. Sketchbook p. 25

4-18: [3,4,7, 10]

In comparing the full score, the duet, and the two sketches (Exx. 3a–3d), one can conclude that the final harmony, 4–18, was the initial and fixed goal of the progression. The variable factor appears to be the bass line, and to some extent, the soprano. The extent to which the bass line was determined by vertical rather than horizontal considerations is problematic. Suffice it to point out that all the verticals in the full score version (Ex. 3a) are significant harmonies in *The Rite of Spring*, whereas in the piano duet score (Ex. 3b) the two middle verticals are sets of little consequence. In the duet version the bass line is 4-Z29, a significant tetrachord (one of the two all-interval tetrachords) in the work, whereas the bass line of the full score version is 4–22, a tetrachord of lesser significance. This evaluation assumes, of course, that Stravinsky was always concerned about the harmonies that underlay linear formations, an assumption that is not consistently verifiable.

The remaining two sketches (Sketchbook p. 26, line 2, m. 4, and p. 27, line 3, m. 3) do not supply any new information except that Stravinsky was still undecided. In the first one the final chord is the same as that in Ex. 3c. In the second the final chord is the same as that in the duet and the full score. In both these sketches the preceding chords are incomplete: Only the two upper notes are given.[5]

5. It is possible, of course, that the first complete score, the duet score, contains uncorrected errors: specifically, that the bass notes E and D lack flat signs. In this

Ex. 4. *Introduction to Part 2:* R84

(4 - 27)   4 - 18 (4 - 27) 4 - 18 (4 - 27) (4 - 27)   4 - 18

In Ex. 4 we have a variant on one of the two main melodic themes of this movement and the main theme of the next movement (*Mystic Circle of the Adolescents*). There are two forms of 4–18 here, one with soprano Ab and one with soprano Gb, [8,9,0,3] and [6,7,10,1]. The two forms are transpositionally related, with $t = 10$, one of the two values of t that yield complete variance (no common pc's). (See Ex. 59 in *StrAM.*)

The Sketchbook provides ample evidence of the time and thought Stravinsky spent perfecting the harmonization of this variant as well as the other two forms of the Khorovod tune. (See Sketchbook pp. 46, 50 53, 55, 59, 62, 64–65, as well as 105–07.)

Ex. 5. *The Chosen One:* R105+2

8 - 18: [0,1, 3, 4, 6, 7, 8, 9]

The total sound configuration in Ex. 5 is 8–18, as indicated. The piano duet differs from the full score in that 8–18 occurs only at R105+2, whereas in the full score it occurs at the beginning of the movement. Conversely, the full score conceals a relation that is clear from the piano duet

---

connection is should be observed that the full score underwent a few revisions after its initial publication in 1921, including a change in this passage. In the course of this change horns 6 and 8 were erroneously assigned a G clef instead of an F clef. The resulting discrepancy between the full score and the duet is even more striking than those discussed, if the clefs are taken literally.

but not immediately relevant to the discussion here: The predominant
hexachord at the beginning of *The Chosen One* is of the same type as the
chord in the 11/4 bar immediately preceding, namely, 6-Z23. (Ex. 69).

These few examples of the recurring sets 4-18 and 8-18 are intended
to support the following general observation: *The Rite of Spring* is unified
not so much by literally repeated formations, although there are a few
instances of this, or by thematic relations of a traditional kind, as by the
underlying harmonic units, that is, by the unordered pc sets, considered
quite apart from the attributes of specific occurrences. In this respect
The Rite of Spring resembles the extraordinary early atonal works of
Schoenberg and his students, and, indeed, from our contemporary vantage
point it has more in common with those works than with the later works
of its composer—in particular, with the so-called neoclassical works, at
least as we understand them now.

The roles of various sets and the relation of the individual movements
to the total work will be considered next.

Chronological Survey of the Work

In this section I will make no attempt to cover such features of the music as tonality, large-scale linear connections, register, or orchestration.

Introduction to Part 1

Although some of the sets introduced here occur prominently elsewhere in the work, many are of only secondary importance with respect to the work as a whole. It seems plausible, after extensive study of *The Rite of Spring*, that this introduction was written at a very early stage, perhaps even before Stravinsky had the outlines of the entire work clearly in mind. Two surface features render this convincing: Nowhere else in the piece is there such an obvious use of familiar diatonic formations together with primitive chromatic progressions. It should be remarked, in this connection, that there are apparently no extended sketches for the *Introduction to Part 1* in the Sketchbook or elsewhere.[6]

R0–R3+6

The famous opening melody (Ex. 6) presents set 6-32 (the major hexachord), which is, of course, the source of many of the diatonic melodic figures that characterize certain parts of the music—notably themes and motives.

Ex. 6. *Introduction to Part 1*

Bn.   6 - 32: [7, 9, 11, 0, 2, 4]

6. Appendix C of Eric W. White's *Stravinsky* (Berkeley: University of California Press, 1966) consists of a "Catalogue of Manuscripts (1904–1952) in Stravinsky's Possession." Two of the items may contain sketches for the *Introduction,* but this cannot be ascertained from the description given.

(Clearly, what Stravinsky wished to express with these diatonic formations is the folk mysticism of the ballet; however, the music in toto is far more complex and quickly breaks out of the sphere of naive diatonicism.)

Ex. 7a. *Introduction to Part 1:* R2

E.H.   4-23: [1,3,6,8]

Ex. 7b. *Introduction to Part 1:* R3+2

E.H.   5-23: [1,3,4,6,8]

The most immediate derivatives of 6-32 are 4-23 at R2 and the expansion of 4-23 at R3+2 to 5-23 (Exx. 7a, 7b). Although 4-23 is contained in 6-32 three times and 5-23 is contained twice, neither melodic ordering of these sets derives directly from the ordering of 6-32; that is, in neither case is the smaller set simply an ordered transformation of some segment of the parent set, 6-32.

Ex. 8. *Introduction to Part 1:* R1+2

Cl.(D)
4-10: [1,3,4,6]   4-10: [11,1,2,4]

Pitch class set 4-10, another offspring of 6-32, comes in at the end of the first long melodic configuration, at R1+2 (Ex. 8). The total set there (6-2) is composed of two overlapping forms of 4-10 as shown (Ex. 8). The single common pitch between the two transpositionally related forms ($t = 10$) is E. (Such melodic configurations are commonplace, of course, in the later serial works of Stravinsky [see *StrAM*, Ex. 76.]) Pitch class set 4-10 is encountered throughout *The Rite of Spring*, primarily in melodies. In the top line of Ex. 2 its ordering identifies it as the traditional minor tetrachord.

Ex. 9. *Introduction to Part 1:* R2+2

4 - 16 : [8,9,1,3]

At R2+3 a more characteristic atonal set, 4–16, serves as the cadential harmony (Ex. 9). This set subsequently assumes an important role elsewhere, for instance, as the ostinato figure in the *Introduction to Part 2* beginning at R86+3 (Ex. 10) and, even more remarkably, as the last chord in the entire work (Ex. 106).

Ex. 10. *Introduction to Part 2:* R86+3

4 - 16: [3,4,8,10]

The end of the section is signaled by the recurrence of 4–12 (Ex. 11), a transposition of the set that closes the bassoon solo at R1+1.

Ex. 11. *Introduction to Part 1:* R3+2

Bn.   4 - 12: [3,6,7,9]

Again, this is a set that occurs in other sections of the music. A prominent instance is shown in Ex. 12, the beginning of *Kiss of the Earth.*

Ex. 12. *Kiss of the Earth:* R71

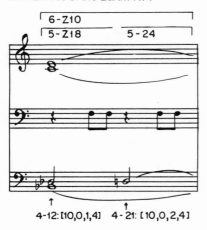

4-12: [10,0,1,4]   4-21: [10,0,2,4]

R4–R6+10

A fixed feature of the first five measures of this section is the 4-note chord sustained by clarinet and horns (Ex. 13).

Ex. 13. *Introduction to Part 1:* R4

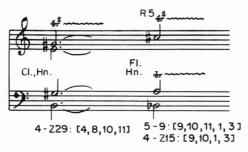

4-Z29: [4,8,10,11]   5-9: [9,10,11, 1, 3]
                    4 - Z15: [9,10,1, 3]

The set is 4-Z29 (the all-interval tetrachord), as indicated. It is succeeded at R5 by 5-9 (Ex. 13), and in the duet score, which lacks the trill on A, by 4-Z15—the other form of the all-interval tetrachord—thus retaining interval content over a change in pc content. This kind of intervallic structuring is far more typical of Schoenberg and Webern, but there is more than one such instance in *The Rite of Spring.*

The main melodic components at R4, pc sets 5-4 and 6-2, are not especially significant elsewhere in the work but derive in an obvious way from the chromatic sets at the beginning of the *Introduction.* The melodic set at R5, 4-17, is another matter. Although it is not especially important in the subsequent music it does play a supportive, secondary role in many passages (see Ex. 44). This set is one of the more familiar atonal tetrachords, the so-called major–minor tetrachord, about which much has been written.[7]

Ex. 14. *Introduction to Part 1:* R5

4-17: [1,4,5,8]

From the first beat at R6 extending through the first quarter note of R6+1 (a new segment of music) is the first statement of 7–31. As will be pointed out several times further on, this set and its complement are basic harmonies in *The Rite of Spring,* together with their subsets. (The pc set in normal order here is [10,11,1,2,4,5,7].)

Ex. 15. *Introduction to Part 1:* R12+7 (Piano Duet)

6-34:[10,0,2,4,6,7]   5-31:[7,10,1,3,4]

3-7

6-27:[10,1,3,4,6,7]

7. Ernest Ansermet (*Les fondements de la musique dans la conscience humaine,* [Neuchâtel: Baconnière, 1961], vol. 2, p. 267) has an informative anecdote concerning Stravinsky's relation to this chord as well as his interest in new "chords": "One evening when we (Ravel, Stravinsky, and I) were discussing the idea that Schoenberg had had of making use of a 'major-minor' chord . . . . Ravel said: 'Of course it is possible, but on the condition that the minor third be placed above and the major third below.' 'If that disposition is possible,' replied Stravinsky, 'I do not see why the inverse is not possible; and if I want it that way, I can do it that way' [*si je le veux, je le peux*]." [author's translation]

As but one instance of a later occurrence of the complement of 7-31 (5-31), Ex. 15 displays it as it occurs at the end of the *Introduction* in the context of 6-27, one of the basic hexachords in *The Rite of Spring*. Notice that the example is drawn from the duet score. Again, there is a discrepancy between that score and the full score. In the latter, pc's 4 and 10 (E and A#) are not part of the sustained chord but are carried by the solo violas and combine with the winds only for the value of one eighth note. Obviously the determining factor in this and other similar situations is orchestration, for at the time Stravinsky prepared the duet score (for the ballet rehearsals) he had not fully completed the orchestration. This is borne out by the Sketchbook, if one can assume that it contains a major portion of the sketches.

The end of this section of the *Introduction to Part 1* is marked by 8-18, as shown in Ex. 1. Both 7-31 and 7-32 (to be discussed below) are in the set-complex relation Kh with 8-18: that is, both are contained in 8-18 and both contain the complement of 8-18 (4-18).

Example 15 shows two other harmonies of interest: 6-27, which occurs in eight of the fourteen movements, often in a vital structural role, and set 6-34, which, although of lesser significance, is interesting since it is of the same type as Scriabin's "mystic chord."

R7-R9+4

This section is essentially a development of the material presented in the opening section of the *Introduction* and hence requires no discussion here, except perhaps to point out that whereas the major hexachord 6-32 played an important part in the opening section, the minor hexachord 6-33 introduced here by alto flute at R9 is important.

R10-R11+3

This penultimate section repeats harmonies of the opening music, including 4-23, as shown in Ex. 16 (cf. Ex. 7a), set out as the predominant melody in D clarinet at R10, associated diatonic formations, and the chromatic derivatives.

Ex. 16. *Introduction to Part 1:* R10

Cl.(D)   4-23

The most extraordinary aspect of this section, however, is the appearance at R10 of pc set 5-32 as the main underlying harmony (Ex. 17a), for it is this event that prepares the main harmony of the forthcoming *Augurs of Spring* (Ex. 17b), the complement of 5-32 (7-32).[8] (Perhaps even more extraordinary is the fact that this prominent harmonic configuration has never before been mentioned in the literature. The *Augurs of Spring* chord, of course, is one harmony mentioned in any discussion of *The Rite of Spring*.)

Ex. 17a. Introduction to Part 1: R10

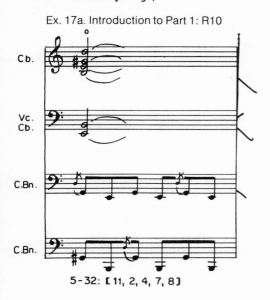

5-32: [11, 2, 4, 7, 8]

Ex. 17b. *Augurs of Spring:* R13

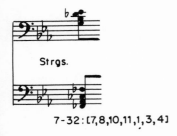

7-32: [7,8,10,11,1,3,4]

R12-R12+9

The primary harmonies of the final section of the *Introduction* have already been discussed in part in connection with Ex. 15. The one set shown there but not commented upon is 3-7, which prepares the forth-

---

8. Set 7-32 in Ex. 17b is not the literal complement of 5-32 in Ex. 17a but is a transposition of the complement of the latter ($t = 10$).

coming *Augurs of Spring* chord in such an obvious way that extended comment hardly seems necessary.[9]

Two further harmonies, nevertheless, require some explanation. First, the C introduced by clarinet at R12+2 combines with the *Augurs of Spring* motive (the set 3–7 shown in Ex. 15) to form 4–10, replicating the diatonic formation in the first section of the *Introduction*. Set 4–10 is expanded to 5–2 in this situation by the inclusion of the embellishing note D in the clarinet trill. Second, the melodic flourish at R12+5 is puzzling at first, for the total set formed is 6–Z48. The full score clarifies. As shown in Ex. 18, the instrumentally determined components of 6–Z48 (otherwise a relatively insignificant set in *The Rite of Spring*) are 4–23 and 4–16, both important sets (Ex. 99b). The total hexachord here is therefore not so crucial as its parts, with respect to the work as a whole.

Ex. 18. *Introduction to Part 1:* R12+5

Augurs of Spring (R13)

R13–R15+5

The *Augurs of Spring* chord (7–32) has already been mentioned and displayed in Ex. 17b. The consequent phrase at R14 introduces new harmonies, which are shown in Ex. 19.

9. In general this study does not deal with trichords, because they are easily identifiable components of larger sets. In this case the trichord 3–7 relates to the immediately following set, 4–23, of which it is a subset (two times). Pitch class set 3–7 is a kind of motto trichord in the work.

Ex. 19. *Augurs of Spring:* R14

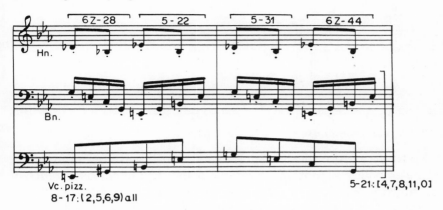

Far from being an arbitrary conflation of major triads in some vague poly-
harmonic sense, the passage forms sets that are of significance in a number
of other parts of the work.[10] Most apparent to the reader on the basis
of the preceding discussion of the *Introduction* will be 8-17 (the complement of 4-17 [Ex. 14]), here the set formed by the total configuration,
and 5-31 (Ex. 15).

The arpeggiations introduced by bassoon and cello form set 5-21, which
is almost maximally different from 5-32 with respect to interval content
and represents a marked sonic contrast to the preceding *Augurs of Spring*
chord. All the harmonies formed within each quarter-note pulse are significant sets, including 5-22, whose complement 7-22 is the often-sited
chord shown in Ex. 49a. In particular, the two hexachords 6-Z28 and
6-Z44 are fundamental harmonies in the last movement, the *Sacrificial
Dance* (see Exx. 88a, 90, 92, 94).

Two additional sets of interest in this section are 4-8 at R15 and 5-1
at R15+2. Pitch class set 4-8 is representative of a number of sets in *The
Rite of Spring*: They occur fairly often but do not have special significance
compared to the more basic sets, such as 5-31. Example 20a shows the
two forms of 4-8 that introduce the chromatic set 5-1 at R15.

10. The duet score is essentially a simplification of the full score for the passage.
Here, as observed earlier, the full score is the basis of the example, unless otherwise
indicated in the example.

Ex. 20a. *Augurs of Spring:* R15

W.W.
Vn.

Ob. ³

Tpt.

4-8:[11,0,4,5]   4-8:[7,8,0,1]   5-1:[6,7,8,9,10]

The two forms are transpositionally related ($t = 8$), with one common note, the embellishing note, C. A later and also prominent occurrence of 4-8 is shown in Ex. 20b, where the set serves to enhance the final statement of the Khorovod tune for that movement and to prepare for the transition to the following movement.

Ex. 20b. *Mystic Circle of the Adolescents:* R101

Strgs.
Fl.

4-8 : [6,7,11,0]

As for 5-1, this is a chromatic set the first instances of which were in the *Introduction to Part 1;* both 5-1 and its relatives (3-1, 4-1, 6-1, and so on) belong almost exclusively to the melodic dimension and do not relate, usually, to the more fundamental harmonies in *The Rite of Spring.*

R16-R17+4
The sets in this section are mainly diatonic, emphasizing 4-10 (the predominant tune), 4-23, and 5-23, sets already discussed in connection with the *Introduction.* Thus, the harmony of the section stands in marked contrast to the opening section of the movement with the ostinato figure forming 3-7 (Ex. 19) and the iterative rhythmic pattern being the constant elements.

R18–R21+9

Again, with one exception, no new sets are introduced. Rather, the section is composed mostly of 7–32 (the *Augurs of Spring* chord) and the diatonic melody 4–10. The exception is the total harmony produced by the combination of these sets, 8–27, a set of some importance in *The Rite of Spring*, while its complement, 4–27, familiar as the dominant seventh and half-diminished seventh chords, is a common component of the Debussy style, which is so evident in many parts of *The Rite of Spring*.

R21+10–R27+7

At R21+10, once again there is a discrepancy between the duet score and the full score. In the duet score the chord that marks the end of one section and the beginning of the next is 6–30: [10,0,1,4,6,7].[11] The D# that follows creates 7–31 (Ex. 21a), so that the new hexachord is introduced in the context of an established harmony, i.e., the subset relation is explicit.

Ex. 21a. *Augurs of Spring:* R21+10 (Piano Duet)

6-30 : [10,0,1,4, 6,7]
7 - 31 : [10,0,1,3,4,6,7]

In the full score, in contrast, the hexachord is 6-Z50 (Ex. 21b) and the following Eb supplies no new pitch-class information; the hexachord is unchanged.

11. This is the same type as the "Petrouchka" chord (see *StrAM*, Ex. 19). The prototype of this harmony is found in the Prologue, Second Tableau, of Mussorgsky's *Boris Godunov*, notated as a combination of an Ab7 and D7 chord.

Ex. 21b. *Augurs of Spring:* R21+10

Strgs.   Hn.,Tbn.

6-Z50: [10,0,1,3,6,7]

6-Z50 is, however, a subset of 7–31, in the abstract. A sketch for this location in the Sketchbook is found on p. 5, a pencil sketch (with no key signature) that is identical to the duet version. It is quite possible that the full-score version contains an error: specifically, that the violas should have E natural and F#, not Eb and F#. This is substantiated by the orchestral sketch on p. 117 of the Sketchbook. Again without key signature, the orthography corresponds to that of the duet. It seems very likely that Stravinsky forgot that the viola E would receive a flat with the key signature.

Ex. 22. *Augurs of Spring:* R25

Solo Hn.
5-23

At R22+2 there is a return to 4–10 within 5–2 as at R12+3, the transition to *Augurs of Spring.* The trill on C is then transposed up a fifth and retarded at R24+3 to become the preparation for the Khorovod tune for this movement, based on 5–23 (Ex. 22), which contains 4–10 as a prominent subset. Thus, the new theme is prepared by a prior statement of the harmony 4–10 as well as by the contextual detail, the trill. In addition, the combination of the retarded trill and the fixed 3-note motive forms the set 4–12 (Ex. 23) (cf. Exx. 11, 12).

Ex. 23. *Augurs of Spring:* R24+4

4-12: [7,9,10,1]

The entire formation shown in Ex. 23 is set 5-28, which is of some significance later in the music. (See Ex. 63c and comments thereon and Ex. 95.)

Ex. 24. *Augurs of Spring:* R26

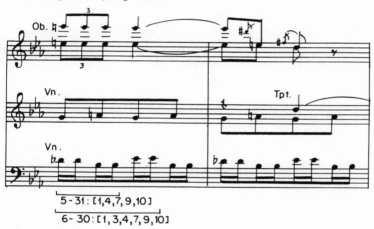

5-31: [1,4,7,9,10]
6-30: [1,3,4,7,9,10]

The onset of the new theme at R26 (Ex. 24), with oboes playing the
octave E, forms 5-31 with the new ostinato figure shown in Ex. 23. When
Eb enters in the ostinato figure, set 6-30 is created, as indicated in Ex. 24.
Comparing this form of 6-30 with the problematic form of 6-30 discussed
in connection with Exx. 21a and 21b, we find that they are transpositionally related, the second being a transposition of the first up three half
steps. This produces the invariant subset 4-28 [1,4,7,10], a set strongly
linked to 5-31. This latter occurrence of 6-30 supports to some extent
the priority of the duet version of the chord at R21+10 (Ex. 21a).

Example 24 does not show the complete texture at R26. An additional
component was introduced at R24+2 and continues through R26: the
tetrachord 4-11: [0,2,4,5]. Remarkably, the total texture then becomes

9-7: (6,8,11), the transformed complement of the motive Bb, Db, Eb.[12]
Large sets of this kind involved in the complement relation (here the complement is embedded) are not unusual in *The Rite of Spring,* although
they are not so pervasive as in Schoenberg's atonal music, or Webern's for
that matter. There is another instance almost immediately, however.

Ex. 25a. *Augurs of Spring:* R27

At R26+6 the music changes again: the 2-note figure G-A becomes Bb-
C (in preparation for the transposed form of the Khorovod tune at R27
[Ex. 25a]) and is doubled a fourth below. Together with the persistent
4-11 [0,2,4,5], this forms 8-10, the complement of 4-10, which was
most recently formed by the melody at R19. These instances of complementation demonstrate the extent to which the components of this music
are interrelated.

R28–R29+7
The accompanying parts at R28 resemble those at R16—a diatonic setting.
At R28+4 a new theme is introduced in counterpoint to the Khorovod
tune, one that is to become the principal theme of *Spring Rounds.*

Ex. 25b. *Augurs of Spring:* R28+4

This theme (Ex. 25b) is based upon 4-10 and derives in an obvious way
from 4-10 as a subset of 5-23 in the Khorovod tune. Examples 25a and
25b are self-explanatory, although in Ex. 25b attention might be directed
to the retrogression involved in the derivation. Such melodic manipula-
tions, of course, are found in *Petrouchka,* as well.

12. For displaying the pc content of 9-7 here, complement notation, as explained
in the introduction, has been used.

R30–R30+7

The most striking new feature of this section is the diminished-seventh chord introduced by violins at R30.

Ex. 26. *Augurs of Spring:* R30

Vn.

4 - 10: [5,7,8,10] 8 - 28: (0,3,6,9)
[11,1,2,4]

As shown in Ex. 26, the horizontal figure is based on 4–10, and the total configuration is 8–28, the complement of the diminished-seventh chord, 4–28.[13] The large set 8–28 is one of the fundamental components in *The Rite of Spring.*

This passage is typical of the way in which Stravinsky combines diverse materials into a meaningful whole. In the duet score, which is less elaborate than the full score at this point, the harmony on each quarter-note at R30 is the set 7–25. Upon first inspection it appears that this degree of regularity does not extend over the entire passage, which perhaps may best be regarded as consisting essentially of two layers, the diatonic part (as at R16) and the diminished seventh component (Ex. 26). Nevertheless, a set-complex reading of the components of the passage reveals that all, including those formed on each quarter-note pulse, are related to the set complex about 4–28 and 8–28, with 6–27 connecting the two totally dissimilar tetrachords, 4–10 and 4–28.[14] The appearance of 6–27 at this juncture is particularly significant in that it is the first appearance of that set since R12+7. Moreover, 6–27 will be the opening harmony of the forthcoming movement, *Ritual of Abduction.*

R31–R36+3

In this final section of the movement no startlingly new elements are introduced. Indeed, the section is primarily diatonic, the only pervasive new components being the trichordal figures in the bass that echo the syncopation established at the beginning of the movement (Exx. 27a, 27b).

---

13. Again, this is hardly surprising since any combination of two disjunct diminished-seventh chords sums to the complement of a diminished-seventh chord.

14. See *StrAM*, p. 114, for a discussion of connectedness within the set complex.

Ex. 27a. *Augurs of Spring:* R31

Ex. 27b. *Augurs of Spring:* R32

From R31 through R31+7 the most prominent harmony is 6–33 (the minor hexachord), which expands to 8–13 (10,1,3,4) with the inclusion of the bass figure shown in Ex. 27a. The sets 8–13 and 4–13 occur in several movements (see Exx. 66a, 71) but are not among the most significant sets in the work. Set 8–13 occurs next in the following movement at R37+2, the last two-thirds of the measure.

From R32 to the end of the movement (R36+3), the overall harmony is still diatonic, comprising the set 7–34, the complement of the ninth chord so familiar in Debussy's music (cf. Ex. 76a).

Ritual of Abduction (R37)

R37–R42+6

Virtually all the harmonies in this movement have been stated previously and are significant over the entire work. This is evident at the very outset, as shown in Ex. 28a. Set 6–27 first occurred at R12+7 in the transition from the *Introduction* to *Augurs of Spring* (Ex. 15) and subsequently appeared in *Augurs of Spring* as discussed above. Comparing the statement of 6–27 at the head of the present movement with the statement at R12+7, we find that the two are transpositionally related, with $t = 9$. This level of transposition produces maximum invariance under that operation (vector [225222]) and the invariant subset is 5–31. The association of this invariant subset with the local harmony becomes clear at R37+1, where the addition of F# (timpani) creates the set 7–31, the complement of 5–31.

Ex. 28a. *Ritual of Abduction:* R37

6-27: [7,10,0,1,3,4]

7-31: [10,0,1,3,4,6,7]

Ex. 28b. *Ritual of Abduction:* R38

6:27: [3,6,8,9,11,0]

Ex. 29. *Ritual of Abduction:* R37+2

Ww.   6-32:[2,4,6,7,9,11]
(Fl.,Ob.,Cl.,Picc.)

Set 6-32 enters at R37+2 (Ex. 29), sounding against the sustained chord 6-27. Although the two strata are essentially detached in the set-complex sense, their juxtaposition produces three harmonies that are found elsewhere: 8-12, 8-13, and 7-31. Set 7-31 appears on the first beat of R37+3 and on the last beat of R37+4, set 8-12 on the last beat of R37+3, and 8-13 on the first beat of R37+4. Two other sets, 9-2 and 8-3, are formed in the same way as those just mentioned but are not significant harmonies elsewhere; hence the passage cannot be said to be completely structured with respect to the verticals formed over the individual pulses (dotted quarter values).

At R38, set 6-27 is transposed (an ordered transposition) and the value of t is 8, one of the eight levels that produce only two invariants. Example 28b shows this new form of 6-27.[15]

Ex. 30. *Ritual of Abduction:* R39

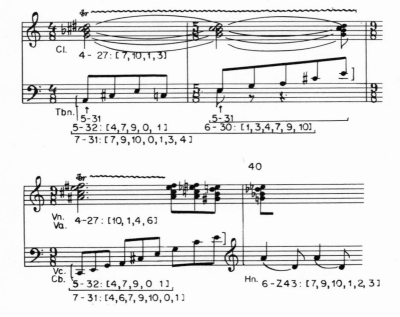

15. The bracketed sharp before F corrects an apparent error in Cl. 2 in the full score.

The subsequent short passage, R39-R39+2, is extraordinary in a number of ways and, accordingly, is shown in full in Ex. 30. Notice, first, the two large sets. Both are forms of 7-31: the first spans the first two measures, the second spans the first part of the third measure. The two forms are transpositionally related, with $t = 9$, one of three levels that produce maximum invariance. In this case (and always for this value of t) the invariant subset is 6-27: [10,1,3,4,6,7], of which more will be said below. Within the first form of 7-31 is the melodic configuration that forms 5-32—and the importance of 7-32 and 7-31 throughout *The Rite of Spring* has already been commented upon. Further analysis of 5-32 in terms of its subsets yields 4-27, which occurs in two adjacent forms in the upper parts, as shown. The remarkable fact here is that the union of these two forms of 4-27 produces 6-27: [10,1,3,4,6,7], exactly the hexachord that is common to the two forms of 7-31 mentioned above. In the second measure of the passage 6-30 is produced by the combination of upper and lower parts, as indicated. By now this is a familiar set (see Exx. 21a, 24), and it only need be remarked that 6-30 is a member of the set complex about 7-31/5-31 (Ex. 110). Indeed, 5-31 is the accented vertical in two instances, as shown in Ex. 30. Finally, at the termination of the passage a new set is formed, 6-Z43. This is the first appearance of this harmony, which plays such an important role in the last movement, the *Sacrificial Dance*.

The section beginning with R42 and extending up to R43 is such an extremely complicated tutti that a representation of the full score is not feasible. For the present purpose, the duet score, which is a simplification of the full score here, may be consulted. A good deal of the complexity disappears, for only three harmonies are involved: 6-27, 7-31, and 8-28. Involved are two strata, represented by Prima and Seconda parts in the duet. Measure 42+1 will suffice to suggest the general scheme: There the Prima part has 7-31: [1,3,4,6,7,9,10], while the Seconda part has 6-27: [9,10,0,1,3,6].

R43-R43+6

The ubiquitous diatonic set, 5-23, is predominant in the upper voice (woodwinds, excluding bassoon), and the texture is representative of what used to be called dissonant counterpoint. Notwithstanding the linear disposition, the small-scale verticals in the passage are significant sets in the main (Ex. 31).

Ex. 31. *Ritual of Abduction:* R43

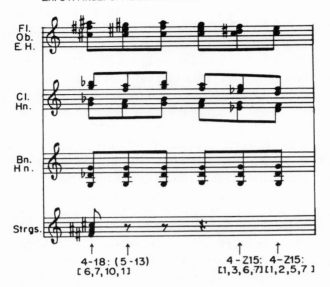

4-18: (5-13)   4-Z15: 4-Z15:
[6,7,10,1]   [1,3,6,7][1,2,5,7]

It will be recalled that sets 4-18 and 4-Z15 are two of the principal tetrachords throughout *The Rite of Spring.*[16] (Set 5-13 is of minimal significance.) Observe that the two successive forms of 4-Z15 shown in Ex. 31
are inversionally related ($t = 8$) about the invariant dyad G-Db.[17]

R44–R45+2

The section begins with a return to the horn motive shown at the end of
Ex. 30. Here, however, the harmonic setting is quite different. There the
hexachord was 6-Z43; here the chord is 5-25 (Ex. 32).

Ex. 32. *Ritual of Abduction:* R44

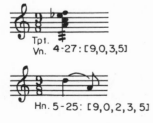

Tpt.
Vn. 4-27: [9,0,3,5]

Hn. 5-25: [9,0,2,3,5]

16. Here and elsewhere it appears that the metrically accented verticals are usually
significant sets. Note the orchestral accent (Ex. 31) with strings on the downbeat only.
These and similar features are lost, of course, in the duet score—one of the reasons
that the examples in the present article are drawn primarily from the full score.

17. The importance of certain fixed single pitches and fixed dyads will not be discussed, although they would not escape the attention of the analyst.

Comparison of Exx. 30 and 32 shows that the variable feature is the sub-set 4–27, but the transposition appears not to be an arbitrary one because 5–25, created by the change, is a subset of 6–27, which dominates the following passage, R44+3–R44+4 (see also Exx. 66a, 100a).

Ex. 33a. *Ritual of Abduction:* R44+3

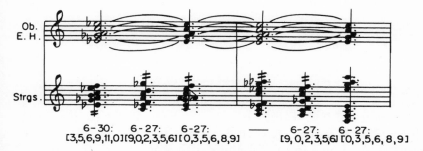

The two ensuing measures, R44+3–R44+4, are composed mainly of a single harmony (Ex. 33a), 6–27, as suggested above. The other set here, 6–30, belongs (with 6–27) to the set complex about 5–31 and 7–31 (and 4–28/8–28), so that the entire passage may be interpreted as an expression of that set, which is so fundamental to the work. In this connection, Ex. 33b shows how 5–31 is formed in the upper voice of the next passage (R45–R46).

Ex. 33b. *Ritual of Abduction:* R45

The most interesting aspect of the passage (Ex. 33a) again has to do with 5–31: The two transpositions of 6–27 are effected with inverse-related values of *t* (3 and 9), which means that the change from one to the other preserves the maximum number of notes (5) and the invariant subset is, of course, 5–31 [9,0,3,5,6]. It should also be remarked that the oboes and English horns hold fixed the set 4–28, which immediately thereafter is given as a line in the topmost voice (Ex. 33b).

Ex. 34. *Ritual of Abduction:* R45

8 - 23: [8,9,10,11,1,3,4,6]

The upper voice of R45–R45+2 has already been discussed in connection with Ex. 33b. It remains to consider the other melodic component of this passage. As shown in Ex. 34, this consists of eight distinct pitches, forming the set 8–23. This large set relates back to 4–23 at R43 and, more immediately, directly ahead to 4–23 at R46+1. The most remarkable feature of this line, however, is its linear substructure: 8–23 contains five forms of 4–23, its complement, and all five are set out as contiguous linear subsets indicated by the brackets above the staff in Ex. 34. That is, any selection of four adjacent notes in the line will yield 4–23.[18]

R46–R47+14

This section is essentially a refrain and closing section for the movement. The entire upper voice is 5–23, incorporating 4–23 as its principal subset. Of special interest in this final section is set 5–16 shown in Ex. 35a.

Ex. 35a. *Ritual of Abduction:* R47

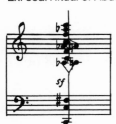

5–16: [5,6,8,9,0]

18. This procedure, which I have called imbrication (in *StrAM*), is used in more arcane ways by Schoenberg in his atonal music. Here, obviously, the progression by fourth and fifth guarantees a uniform substructure.

The Sketchbook (p. 30) indicates that this was originally to have marked the beginning of the new section (Ex. 35b).

Ex. 35b. Sketchbook p. 30

5-16

Example 35b also suggests that the section was originally to have begun with the music now at R47, so that the present section from R46 to R46+7 may be regarded as a later expansion. At any event, 5-16 and its complement are sharply contrasted to the melodic component (5-23 and 4-23) in this passage, both in the surface texture of the music and in the abstract (for the set-complex relations between the sets are minimal). Set 5-16 is initially stated, as remarked above, at R47. It recurs at R47+5 in the same pc form [5,6,8,9,0] and orchestral disposition. Two measures later at R47+7 it is expanded by one note to become 6-15: [4,5,6,8,9,0] (a prominent vertical in the section that begins at R54 [see Ex. 58]), and finally, at R47+12, another note is added to the vertical formation (Ex. 36), creating 7-16, the complement of 5-16—a beautiful example of Stravinsky's idiomatic manner of harmonic development and an instance of embedded complement, of which there are many in the atonal literature. The last added note is, of course, Eb, which becomes the first note of the next movement, *Spring Rounds.*

Ex. 36. *Ritual of Abduction:* R47+12

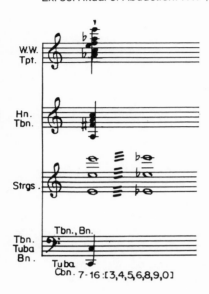

Spring Rounds (R48)

R48-R48+5

This introduction passage is uncomplicated. It is entirely diatonic, consisting of 6-32 (the major hexachord) and its subsets.

R49-R52+5

Again, a diatonic section from the harmonic standpoint. The main harmony is 7-35, which in this ordering would probably be interpreted by most readers as a Dorian mode. Transformations of this set are uncomplicated. Indeed, there is only one in this section: at R49+3, 7-35 is transposed (with $t = 7$) to accompany the consequent melodic phrase, based on 6-33. This transposition produces maximum invariance, the invariant subset being 6-32.

At R50 the chief theme of the movement enters. This is the theme first introduced in *Augurs of Spring* at R28+4 and shown in Ex. 25b. The set is 4-10.

R53-R53+10

This section is considerably more complex harmonically and may be regarded as a development of the previous section, as suggested previously.

It begins, as shown in Ex. 2, with the subset 4–18 playing a prominent role.[19] Although many of the individual verticals are sets that occur elsewhere in the work, they seem to be less important than the horizontal subsets and the fixed vertical subsets of type 4–18. A set-complex view of the section supports this interpretation: Relations between sets are sparse, except for the fact that 4–18 is a subset of every set represented. The cadential harmony of the section, however, is the elemental 5–32, which is sustained while the upper voice melody is completed (Ex. 37).

Ex. 37. *Spring Rounds:* R53+10

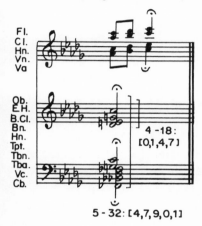

R54–R55+5

This section is a modified version of the last section of the previous movement (*Ritual of Abduction*): the subset of the main melodic component at R47 (4–23) is shortened and transposed ($t = 2$), and the chords 5–16 and 6–15 discussed in connection with that section are also transposed, with $t = 7$. The reason for these particular transpositions is not readily apparent although in the latter case minimal invariance is achieved. The melodic component was originally untransposed with respect to R47 (see Sketchbook, p. 7).

The passage at R55–R55+1 is enigmatic from the harmonic standpoint. The Sketchbook provides no clues, for the one sketch of the passage (p. 10) is virtually identical to the final version except for a difference in barlines and meter and the fact that the last bass note is E, not F. The upper-voice minor third clearly refers to the melody that introduces the movement

19. The first notation of the theme in the Sketchbook (p. 6) gives it together with the descending forms of 4–18.

at R48. But the passage is entirely isolated, never repeated. The verticals on each quarter-note pulse are 4–7: [3,4,7,8]; 5–30: [4,5,8,10,0]; 5–3: [3,4,5,7,8]; and 4–8: [11,0,4,5]. None has particular significance in this context, and only 4–7 and 4–8 are of any importance in the work as a whole (Exx. 20a, 44). If the supporting chords are detached from the horn motive Bb-Ab-Cb, the hexachord 6–14 is obtained: [0,3,4,5,7,8]. But, again, this is a set of no local or broader significance. The only con-figuration that makes sense here is the combination of the melodic upper voices (picc., alto fl., hn., tpt., vn.). These form 5–16, as shown in Ex. 38.

Ex. 38. *Spring Rounds:* R55

5–16: [4,7,8,10,11]

Although this reading is admittedly problematic, 5–16 is the accented sonority in this passage and is contained in 6–15, as in the corresponding section in *Ritual of Abduction* discussed above (Ex. 36).

One further aspect of the section requires attention: the opening of the section (*vivo*) at R54. The 3-note figure played by flute and piccolo combines with the following accented chord (5–16) to form 7–31 (Ex. 39).

Ex. 39. *Spring Rounds:* R54

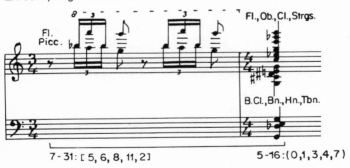

7–31: [5, 6, 8, 11, 2]   5–16:(0,1,3,4,7)

Since this immediately follows the occurrence of 5–32 at R53+10 (Ex. 37), the association of 5–31, 5–32, and 5–16 is emphasized, an association that is evident throughout *The Rite of Spring*. A word of comment upon the relation between the three sets is in order here even though it antici-pates to some extent the summary at the end of this study. All three sets contain a common subset, namely, 4–18, which plays a major role in the work, as is evident from the previous discussion. In addition, 5-32 and 5-16 are maximally similar with respect to interval content, sharing four vector entries (the relation $R1^{20}$). And at a still more fundamental level they all belong to the set-complex K about 8-28/4-28. Moreover, the hexachord 6-27 not only contains all three but is a subset of the larger complement of each. Thus, the three are representative of a family of sets that serve to unify *The Rite of Spring* in the general harmonic sense that is the subject of this study.

R56–R56+7
This final section presents no new music but repeats the introduction to the movement at R48.

Ritual of Two Rival Tribes (R57)

R57–R58+5
Set 4-6, which opens the movement (R57–R57+1), is a new sonority in the work, except for a negligible occurrence of its complement in the *Introduction to Part 1*. It is not significant elsewhere in the work. From the Sketchbook it appears that this brief introduction was an after-thought: The first entry for the passage is a pencil sketch on p. 20, eight pages after the first sketches for the movement (p. 12).

Ex. 40. Sketchbook p. 12

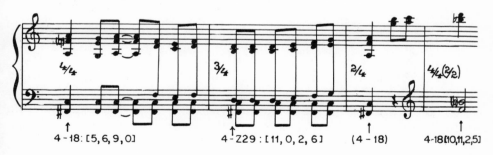

4-18: [5, 6, 9, 0]   4-Z29 : [11, 0, 2, 6]   (4 - 18)   4-18[10,11,2,5]

Sketchbook p. 12 also provides some clarification of the principal music at the opening of the movement (R57+2). As shown in Ex. 40 the original idea was considerably simpler than the final version (which corresponds to the sketch on p. 24 of the Sketchbook). In the final version the line beginning on A is doubled a tenth below ($t = 9$) and the line beginning

20. See introduction.

on F is doubled a sixth below ($t = 4$). This is shown in Ex. 41a, which also lists the sets formed by the individual lines: 5-Z12 and 5-23.

Ex. 41a. *Ritual of two Rival Tribes:* R57+2

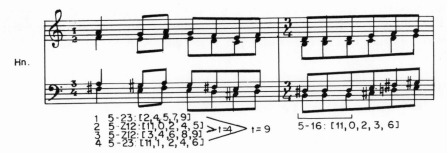

Whereas 5-23 is a familiar set in the music by this time, 5-Z12 has made only one incidental appearance, in *Augurs of Spring* at R22. Its function as a counterpoint to 5-23 may be incidental in this situation. However, 5-Z12 is the Z-correspondent[21] of 5-Z36, which certainly does not have an incidental role in this movement. It is the basis of the theme that enters at R64 (Ex. 41b) and that becomes the main theme of the following movement, *The Procession of the Sage.* The association of 5-Z12 and 5-Z36 in this case may well be accidental, but nevertheless it is a demonstrable relation in the music.[22]

Ex. 41b. *Ritual of two Rival Tribes:* R64

The sketch of R57+2 in Ex. 40 shows that certain metrically accented chords are now-familiar sets, especially 4-18. This feature of *The Rite of Spring* was mentioned above and is particularly well illustrated by the final version of the music. At R57+2 (Ex. 41a) the first three eighths in horns with C and F# in bassoons (not in Ex. 41a) form the elemental set 5-16, which is formed again immediately in the next measure. This regularity prepares for the cadence at R58+5, which has already been discussed in connection with Ex. 3. However, the music that follows the cadence immediately has not been discussed, but it is of great interest (Ex. 42).

21. The term Z-correspondent is explained in the introduction.
22. Again, this is a feature that would not be unusual in the atonal music of Schoenberg.

Ex. 42. *Ritual of two Rival Tribes:* R58+6

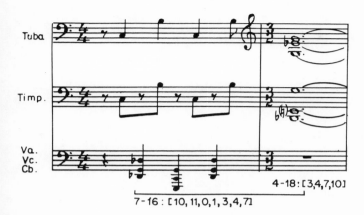

First, the large set 7–16 is formed by the concatenation of the modified opening figure and the restatement of 4–18. Originally (Sketchbook p. 28) this passage was to have consisted only of a literal restatement of the first two measures followed by a return to the music at R57+2. Here it appears that the transposition of the tritone from C-F# (R57) to Db-G (R58+6) was made precisely in order to form the large harmony 7–16, which plays a vital part throughout the music, as has been pointed out.

R59–R59+6

The significance of accented harmonies mentioned above applies also to the new verticals effected by the change of the lower trichord from C-F# (at R57+2) to D#-A at R59.

Ex. 43. *Ritual of two Rival Tribes*

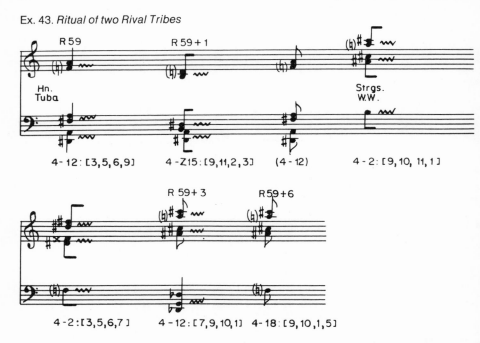

Example 43 shows that the new tetrachords are 4-12 and 4-Z15, compared with 4-18 and 4-Z29 at R57+2 (Ex. 40). The correspondence of 4-Z15 and 4-Z29 is evident: they are the two forms of the all-interval tetrachord and hence have the same interval content. The correspondence of 4-12 and 4-18 is also close: they are maximally similar with respect to interval content (R1).[23] Set 4-12 is, of course, one of the more important sets in *The Rite of Spring* (see, for instance, Exx. 12, 23).

This pattern of significant accented harmonies is broken, however, with the onset of the transposition of 5-23 and its accompanying parts in R59+1 ($t = 4$), where 4-2 becomes the accented vertical (Ex. 43). Set 4-2 is not an especially significant set in *The Rite of Spring* and has no particular meaning in the present movement. At the end of this motion, nevertheless, at R59+3, the accented vertical is again 4-12, and at the end of the repetition of the passage in R59+6 the accented vertical is 4-18. Thus, for the most part, the accented verticals are important and related sets.

The leading melodic voice remains 5-23 (Ex. 41a) until the end of the

23. They are also maximally similar with respect to pitch, but the relation Rp is weakly represented here. Further, both are subsets of the important sets 5-16 and 5-31, which are more than familiar to the reader at this point.

passage at R59+6. However, the accompanying voice changes at R59+1 from 5-Z12 to 5-6, a change that is hardly noticeable because the pattern of thirds between the leading and accompanying voices is maintained. Set 5-6 is related to 5-Z12 in the following way: Both belong to the set complex about 6-Z3 and the set complex about 4-8. The latter is perhaps the more significant abstract connection between the two.

R60–R60+6

A contrasting theme based on 4-10 enters at R60 and returns at R61 and R64, transposed in the last two instances. Again, as shown in Ex. 44, the accented verticals are significant sets. Moreover, 4-7 is maximally similar to 4-17 (R1), differing with regard only to interval classes 1 and 3. In addition, 4-17 and 4-18 are maximally similar (R2) and therefore are in the same relation as 4-12 and 4-18 at R59 (Ex. 43). Set 4-8 remains somewhat anomalous here because it does not fit into the similarity scheme, but its relation to 5-6 (mentioned above) will be recalled.

Ex. 44. *Ritual of two Rival Tribes:* R60

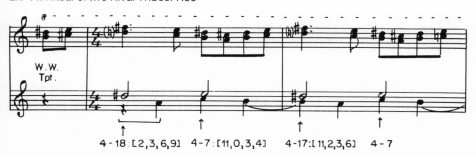

4-18 : [2,3,6,9] 4-7 : [11,0,3,4] 4-17 : [11,2,3,6] 4-7

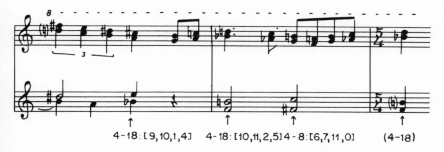

4-18 : [9,10,1,4] 4-18 : [10,11,2,5] 4-8 : [6,7,11,0] (4-18)

Two general comments are in order here. First, although the passage is not structured in terms of functional harmony, it does exhibit a considerable degree of homogeneity in terms of intervallically similar sets. Second, voice-leading appears to be controlled to a large extent by these verticals—and in this respect the passage resembles many in Webern's atonal music.

At R60+4, 4-18 returns in the same form as at R57+2 (Ex. 40). The downbeat of the next measure brings in the fundamental set 5-16, which, as noted above, contains both 4-18 and 4-12, thus preserving the regularity of accented related harmonies.

R61-R61+6

This passage consists of the theme introduced at R60, here transposed, with $t = 8$ (as in the next-to-last measure of Ex. 44) and with a new accompanying part.

Ex. 45. *Ritual of two Rival Tribes:* R61

7 – 31: [6, 8, 9, 11, 0, 2, 3]

It is the latter that is of greatest interest, for the set formed by the accompanying part is 7-31 (Ex. 45).[24] This sonority (based upon one of the fundamental harmonies of the work, as the reader will recall) literally absorbs many of the previous sets, for it contains 4-10, 4-12, 4-Z15, 4-16, 4-17, 4-18, and 4-Z29—all germane to the previous music of this movement.

At R61+3 the upper parts are transposed ($t = 5$) and the accompanying parts inverted to yield 7-31 again: [5,6,8,9,11,0,2].[25] The value of t here is one of four that, under inversion followed by transposition, will yield an invariant hexachord. In the present case the invariant hexachord is of type 6-Z23, which, although not an explicit set here, is the main hexachord in *Honoring of the Chosen One,* entering first in the famous 11/4 measure at R103+1 (Ex. 69).

24. In the Sketchbook p. 25, this accompanying part lacks A (Cl.), so that the set is 6-Z49. If one regards the D in the trill as an embellishing and hence secondary, note, the set is again one of the basic harmonies, 5-32: [3,6,8,11,0]. It seems likely that this was the harmony originally intended for this location in the music.

25. This more sophisticated procedure, involving transposition *and* inversion, is more typical of Part 2 of *The Rite of Spring* than Part 1.

R62–R63+15

The section begins with a statement of 5-16 (Ex. 46) that spans two measures.

Ex. 46. *Ritual of two Rival Tribes:* R62

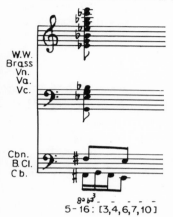

5-16: [3,4,6,7,10]

This is followed by a variant on the first theme, 4-11, replacing 4-10, and then at R62+5 by the hexachord 6-Z50, which dominates the remainder of the section (Ex. 47).

Ex. 47. *Ritual of two Rival Tribes:* R62+7

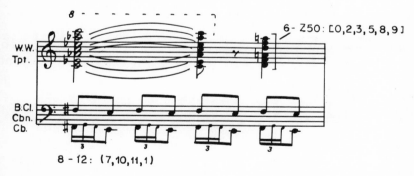

6- Z50: [0,2,3,5,8,9]

8 - 12: (7,10,11,1)

Set 6-Z50 is not a new set in the music (Ex. 21b) and is prominent in the final movement as well, together with its complement, 6-Z29 (Ex. 90). Here it occurs within the large set 8-12, which relates back to its complement at R59 (Ex. 43). But its principal source is probably 7-31, of which it is a subset. In addition, the complement of 6-Z50 (6-Z29) is a subset of 7-32. The significance of these relations is substantiated by later events in the work.

At R63+10, the spectacular orchestral trill, there is a discrepancy between the full score and the piano duet score. The duet score here gives the bass trill as F#-G#, changing at this point from the bass trill E-F# initiated at R62.[26] This creates the large set 8-13: (10,1,3,4). The full score retains the bass trill E-F# at this point, forming the set 8-23: (8,10, 1,3). The 8-23 sonority seems more effective here since it prepares for the subsequent statement of 8-23 at R65.

R64–R66+2

In this final section of the movement *Ritual of Two Rival Tribes*, the most prominent feature is the theme carried by tubas in octaves (Ex. 41b) against a transposition of the contrasting theme first introduced at R60 (Ex. 44). The strongest connection between this theme, based on 5-Z36, and the passage shown in Ex. 44 is 4-18, which is a subset of 5-Z36. The relation remains somewhat abstract, however, because 4-18 as it occurs in 5-Z36 here is G,F#,Bb,C# (not a contiguous subsegment of the theme). The set 5-Z36 is represented by its complement 7-Z36 in the first two measures of the duet version of *Honoring of the Chosen One* (R104– R104+1), where it is formed by all the pitches including the embellishing notes. In the full score at this point the sum of all the pitches is 8-18, which substantiates the observation just made concerning the relation between 5-Z36 and 4-18.

Ex. 48. *Introduction to Part 2:* R86

Tpt

6-Z17 : [4, 5, 8, 10, 11, 0]

At R65, pitch A is added to the sonority by alto flute, oboe, and English horn. Assimilated to the diatonic theme and its accompanying part it forms the large set 8-23, mentioned above. At R65+2 the horns enter with octave D, which associates with the tuba theme to form 6-Z17: [6,7, 8,10,1,2]. This is the last set to sound in the movement (R66–R66+2). Whereas the new set 8-23 is not unfamiliar, 6-Z17, except for a brief appearance in the *Introduction to Part 1* and in *Spring Rounds*, has not been

26. Sketchbook p. 16 also gives F#-G#.

a prominent set. Certainly its most outstanding role is in the *Introduction to Part 2* at R86 (Ex. 48). Its complement, 6-Z43, is more important, especially in the *Sacrificial Dance* (see also Ex. 30).

Procession of the Sage (R67)

R67–R70+8 (all [no sections])
Although short, this is a very complicated movement.[27] The predominant melodic component is the tuba theme (5-Z36) continued from the previous movement. A detailed discussion of the passage from R70 to R70+3 is given in *StrAM* (pp. 85–89). This passage will serve as representative of the harmonic content of the movement for the purpose of the present study; the main features are summarized below.

Perhaps the most remarkable aspect of the passage is the degree of regularity found in the vertical composite segments. The following lists illustrate:

Quarter-note segments	Successive half-note segments
*5-28	8-28
5-31/7-31	8-18
*7-Z38	(9-10)
6-27	(12-1)
*6-Z28	
6-30	
8-12	

Of course, such a list is not very meaningful without specifying relations among the sets (which will be done below). First, a few comments on some of the sets. The sets marked by an asterisk will be relatively unfamiliar to the reader who has followed the discussion this far, and indeed, none of these sets is of great importance elsewhere although all occur in other movements. Set 5-28 plays a role in *The Mystic Circle of the Adolescents* at R86+3, 7-Z38 occurs in the *Introduction to Part 2*,[28] and 6-Z28, which first occurred in *Augurs of Spring* (Ex. 19), is a strong component in the *Sacrificial Dance*. In the second column above, two sets (9-10 and 12-1 [the total chromatic]) are omitted from the present discussion. For the record, set 9-10 relates to both 8-note sets listed there, and 12-1 is uninteresting.

27. The relevant Sketchbook page (17) is one of the more difficult pages to decipher. It differs in a number of ways from the final version.
28. The Z-correspondent of the complement of 7-Z38 (5-Z18) is significant in *Honoring of the Chosen One* at R112+3.

Graphs 1 (top) and 2 (bottom)

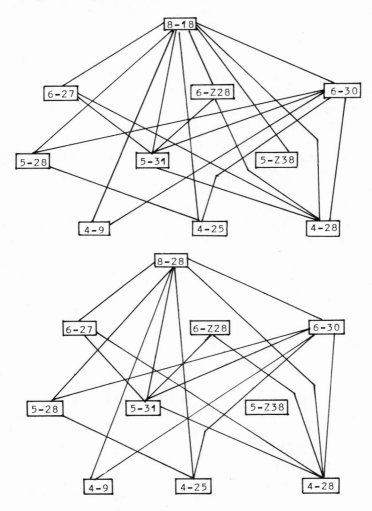

In addition to the sets listed above as composite segments, three tetrachords are especially important in the detail of the passage: 4-9, 4-25,
and 4-28. Of these, 4-28 is most important throughout *The Rite of Spring*.

The inclusion relations among the sets mentioned above are summarized
in graphs 1 and 2, with the largest sets at the top of the graphs in each
case.[29] In general the diagrams dramatize the extent to which these sets

29. A line connecting a larger set with a smaller indicates that the larger set contains
the smaller.

are interrelated to form a cohesive harmonic structure. The 8–18 diagram is especially interesting in this respect because the large set (8–18) has connectors to every other set in the diagram. Indeed, it has the only connection to 5-Z38. Although 5–31 has five connectors, 6–30, surprisingly, has the greatest number of connectors after 8–18. (Instances of this important set are shown in Exx. 21a, 24, 30, 33a.)

The 8–28 diagram shows somewhat sparser relations for the largest set, seven connectors in all, while its complement, 4–28, has five. For the other sets in the diagram, relations are generally sparser than they are in the 8–18 diagram. The union of the two diagrams would of course reveal an even more elaborate interaction of the main components.

Kiss of the Earth (R71)

R71–R71+3 (all [no sections])

This is the shortest movement in *The Rite of Spring* and, in fact, should perhaps be considered as the termination of the previous movement (*Procession of the Sage*). From the harmonic standpoint the movement is very peculiar: The number of harmonies is small, and one would expect all of them to be significant, at least with respect to the movements on either side. This, however, is not the case.

Ex. 49a. *Kiss of the Earth:* R71+3 (Piano Duet)

7-22: [6,7,8,11,0,2,3]

The movement ends with set 7-22 (Ex. 49a), the only occurrence of the set in the work, although its complement occurs elsewhere, e.g., in Ex. 19.[30] With reference to the previous movement as well as to the work as a whole, set 7-22 relates most strongly to 8-18, of which it is one of the eight 7-note subsets, along with such fundamental sets as 7-16, 7-31, and 7-32. Notwithstanding, its similarity to those sets (either pitch similarity or interval similarity) is minimal.

Ex. 49b. Sketchbook p. 15

6- 30 : [5, 7, 8, 11, 1, 2]

The Sketchbook page for the movement (15) is very interesting. The first three measures are notated in ink exactly as in the final version. Stravinsky then writes 7-22, strikes it out, and rewrites it, changing the G-sharps to A-flats. Following this is a pencil sketch of another chord with approximately the same registration. The set in this case (Ex. 49b) is 6-30, which, as has been shown, is a structurally significant set in the previous movement. Set 6-30 does not relate to 7-22 in any direct way; it is not a subset of 7-22 and does not contain 5-22. As is demonstrated in the diagrams above, however, 6-30 is a subset of 8-18 and thus shares a common origin with 7-22

The remainder of the movement is summarized in a previous example (Ex. 12). Of the five harmonies that occur there, only 4-12 has an immediate association with the previous movement, through its complement 8-12. Set 4-21, one of the whole-tone tetrachords (with 4-24 and 4-25),

30. The chord in Ex. 49a greatly interested Ernest Ansermet, who apparently endowed it with mystical significance, for he writes "Et l'accord ainsi posé représente sans doute le maximum de tension harmonique que puisse se signifier la conscience musicale" (*Les Fondements de la musique dans la conscience humaine* [Neuchâtel: Baconnière 1961], vol. 2, p. 187).

occurs elsewhere in the work and is especially prominent in the next move-ment (*Dance of the Earth*). Set 6-Z10 is not an important set in *The Rite of Spring*, and its structural role here should be interpreted with respect to 4–12, which it contains, and 8–12, of which it is a subset. Set 5-Z18, to which reference was made in the discussion of the previous movement, belongs to the set complex (Kh) about 4–18/8–18 (cf. Exx. 73, 81). Set 5–24 remains an anomaly: this is its only occurrence in the entire work.

Dance of the Earth (R72)

R72–R78+5 (all [no sections])
Example 50 shows the opening configuration of the movement. This con-sists of the accented chord, 4-Z29, sounding against the ostinato figure that forms 4–21.

Ex. 50. *Dance of the Earth:* R72+2

4-Z29 : [0, 4, 6, 7]

4 - 21 : [6, 8, 10, 0]

The sum of 4-Z29 and 4–21 here is the hexachord 6–21, which is not a major component of the music of *The Rite of Spring*. Nevertheless, both set 4-Z29 and its Z-correspondent, 4-Z15, are characteristic tetrachords in the work, as observed earlier, although not so prominent as others. Set 4-Z29, for instance, has a cadential role in *Mystic Circle of the Adolescents* at R92+2 (Ex. 62). And 4-Z15 is one of the main components of the sub-sequent music at R99 (Ex. 66a).

The opening harmony persists until R73+3 (with secondary formations 7–34 and 6–34 in the upper parts at R72+5 and R73, respectively). At R73+3 the harmony that is to be the final one of the movement (6-Z49) is introduced (Ex. 51).

Ex. 51. *Dance of the Earth:* R73+3

6-Z49: [3,4,6,7,10, 0]

Although 6-Z49 has very few relations to the other sets in its immediate environment, apart from containing 4-Z29, it relates very directly to certain of the more basic harmonies: One of its four 7-note supersets is 7-31, and 5-16 and 5-32 are two of its three 5-note subsets.[31] It is also in the set complex (Kh) about 4-18/8-18. Set 6-Z49 is not especially prominent elsewhere in the work; its complement, 6-Z28, however, is the opening sonority in the *Sacrificial Dance* (R142, Ex. 88a).

Ex. 52. *Dance of the Earth:* R75+4

4 - 10:[10, 0, 1, 3]

The Eb-Bb figure introduced by horn at R73+3 (Ex. 51) develops into set 4-10 at R75+4 (Ex. 52), and this familiar diatonic figure remains until the end, together with its transposed replica, introduced at R75+9.[32] The set has very few relations to the other sets in the movement.

31. In Ex. 51, 5-16 is formed by the new note Eb (Hn.) and 4-Z29 in the upper register.
32. The ordering of set 4-10 here resembles that of 4-10 as a subset of 5-23 at R94 (*The Mystic Circle of the Adolescents*). The association is probably trivial, however (Also cf. Ex. 25a).

Ex. 53. *Dance of the Earth:* R75+6

A new set, 5-10, enters at R75+6, played by trumpet and violin (Ex. 53). The only other important occurrence of the set is at R131 in *Ritual of the Ancestors* (Ex. 77), where it is the basis for the well-known alto flute melody. As is the case with many of the sets in this section, 5-10 has few relations with others in its local surroundings although it does contain 4-10 prominently as [5,7,8,10]. Once again, however, it does relate strongly to some of the fundamental harmonies that occur throughout *The Rite of Spring.* For instance, it is one of the five 5-note subsets of 6-27. (The others are 5-16, 5-25, 5-31, and 5-32.)

From R75+6 through R77+9 the three components 4-10, 5-10, and 4-21 are combined to form a massive 11-note sonority; only one pc is excluded, pc9, which is the foremost single pc at the opening of the following movement, *Introduction to Part 2.*

Introduction to Part 2 (R79)

With respect to the sets used, this movement exhibits greater diversity than any movement other than *Mystic Circle of the Adolescents* and *Sacrificial Dance.* This diversity may be taken as a rough index of complexity, and, indeed, Part 2 altogether is not only more complex than most of Part 1 but also more advanced with respect to compositional procedure.

The *Introduction* is perhaps the most sophisticated of all the movements in Part 2 in a number of ways, but especially with regard to the control of vertical succession. The verticals consist almost exclusively of sets that are significant throughout the work, as will be demonstrated. The sketches, some of which will be cited below, are revealing in this connection, and a few general comments on them are appropriate here.

The sketches for the *Introduction to Part 2* are scattered to some extent in the Sketchbook, suggesting that the *Introduction* required more rethinking than some of the other movements for which the sketches are on more or less consecutive pages of the Sketchbook.[33] For example, the earliest passage drafted for R80 appears on p. 107, whereas the cello solo at R90+3, which concludes the movement, is sketched on p. 50 and is the first sketch for this movement in the Sketchbook. Unfortunately, there are no sketches for the opening music.

R79–R83+4

The movement opens in an extraordinary way, with two successive forms of 6-Z19 (Ex. 54).[34] In this way a single harmony governs the opening music. The transposition here ($t = 11$) holds three pc's invariant, and they comprise the trichord D-F-A, played by horns and oboes.

This is the first important appearance of 6-Z19. It occurs numerous times in the course of the movement and plays a significant role in the last movement, *Sacrificial Dance,* as well, together with its complement, 6-Z44.[35] The set is one of the hexachords of 7-32, and this inclusion relation is especially interesting in the context of the movement since 6-Z19 is very often in the same local environment as 5–32 (Ex. 55).[36]

The large 8-note sonority at the end of the opening music (Ex. 54) is 8-27.[37] The complement of this set, 4-27, is very prominent in the next three sections of the movement (see Ex. 4).

As an illustration of the regularity exhibited by the verticals in this movement, consider Ex. 55.[38]

---

33. The reader who wishes to examine the sketches for the movement will find them on the following pages: 50–51, 60, 62–65, and 104–07. It should be said, however, that the sketch pages (as in the case of many of the Beethoven sketchbooks) may not be correctly collated.

34. Also appears in Ex. 39 in *StrAM*.

35. Both sets are very characteristic of Schoenberg's atonal music.

36. Set 5–32, of course, is a subset of the complement of 6-Z19 (6-Z44).

37. In the duet score the vertical at this point is 7-31 and the vertical on the following eighth note is 5–32. The entire fourth beat is 8-28: (0,3,6,9).

38. See also *StrAM*, Ex. 45.

Ex. 54. *Introduction to Part 2:* R79

Ex. 55. *Introduction to Part 2:* R81+1

The following list gives the sets that correspond to the numbers at the bottom of the example.

1. 6-Z19: [2,3,5,6,9,10]
2. 5-32:   [8,9,0,2,5]
3. 6-Z19: [2,3,5,6,9,10]
4. 7-Z38: [1,2,4,5,7,8,9]   (6-Z19: [1,2,4,5,8,9])
5. 6-Z19: [2,3,5,6,9,10]
6. 5-21:   [9,10,1,2,5]
7. 6-Z25: [2,4,5,7,9,10]
8. 6-30:   [8,9,11,2,3,5]

Of the sets listed, two have already been discussed, 6-Z19 and 5-32. The fourth vertical, 7-Z38, incorporates the melodic note G; excluding that note, the set becomes 6-Z19, as indicated. Set 5-21, the sixth vertical, is a subset of 6-Z19. The set formed on the seventh vertical, 6-Z25 (cf. Ex. 56b), is one of the seven 6-note subsets of 7-32, and the set 6-30 on the last vertical (familiar elsewhere [Exx. 21a, 24, 30, 33a, 49b]) is a subset of 7-31.

Ex. 56a. Sketchbook p. 104

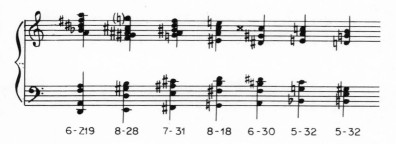

6-Z19   8-28   7-31   8-18   6-30   5-32   5-32

The sketch on Sketchbook p. 104 provides some insight concerning Stravinsky's original conception of the passage from R82 to R83.[39] As shown in Ex. 56a the passage was originally a series of chords, with bass and soprano moving in contrary motion. This succession was greatly expanded in the final version. For example, the first bass note (D) holds for two measures, with changes of chord on each eighth note. And although there is some correspondence of the verticals at the change of bass note in the final version and the verticals in the sketch, those too undergo revision, mostly by the addition or subtraction of one or two notes of the original skeletal harmonies; for example, the vertical above bass note B in the final version is 6-Z50, [7,8,11,1,2,4] while in the sketch it is 5-32: [11,2,4,7,8], the difference being pc1. And, of course, the outer voices of the final version differ from those of the sketch: in the sketch the soprano and bass are 7-35 and 7-27, while in the final version they are 6-Z25 and 6-32, as shown in Ex. 56b.

Ex. 56b. *Introduction to Part 2:* R82-R83

6 - Z25: [1, 2, 4, 6, 7, 9]

6- 32 : [2, 4, 6, 7, 9, 11]

The change for the final version of the soprano has to do with the goal of the soprano voice, which is C#, the note that begins the next statement

39. An additional and interesting aspect of this sketch is discussed below in connection with R161 in the *Sacrificial Dance.*

of the Khorovod tune at R83. The resulting set, however, is 6-Z25, which is one of the hexachords of 7-32 and is also significant as a harmony (Exx. 55, 80, 93). The bass of the final version, 6-32, is a subset of the bass of the sketch, 7-35. Both 6-32 and 7-35 of course, are diatonic.

R84-R85+2
This section presents a variant of the Khorovod tune that is harmonized with 4-27 and 4-18 exclusively, as shown in Ex. 4 (Ex. 59 in *StrAM*). Example 57 shows the three variants on the tune.

Ex. 57

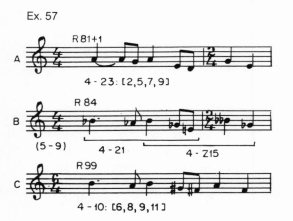

Variant B, which occurs only at R84, is interesting not so much for the total set that it forms (5-9, which is not particularly significant in the work) but for the tetrachords it contains. As shown they consist of 4-21 (whole tone) and 4-Z15 (all interval), both important in the total work. There are no sketches for this variant in the Sketchbook. There are, however, a number of sketches for the other variants, especially for variant C, which occurs only at R99 in the following movement. Some of them will be discussed in connection with that music.

To return to the verticals in Ex. 4, the role of 4-18 in the work has been pointed out a number of times; however, the role of 4-27 (one form of which is familiar in tonal music as the dominant seventh chord) has not been made clear. Set 4-27 is a subset of several of the more fundamental harmonies in the work: 6-27, 5-31, 8-18, 8-28, and 5-32. It is the association with the latter set that is in the foreground in the present movement, and this becomes evident in the music that begins at R87 (see Ex. 60).

The accompanying figure at R84 (not shown in Ex. 4), which consists of the dyad F-Gb stated linearly over three octaves by the lower strings, has primarily a motivic role here, preparing for the motive at R84+3 (Ex. 58). This association becomes explicit with the closing music of the movement (Ex. 61a), when the Bb-Cb dyad (Ex. 58) becomes F-Gb. As the dyad F-Gb interacts with the harmonized melody, however, the harmonies formed are not entirely arbitrary: they include both 5–31 and 5–32.

Ex. 58. *Introduction to Part 2:* R84+3

At R84+3 the second important thematic element of the movement is introduced (Ex. 58). The set formed here is 6–15, which has occurred before in the music, e.g., at R47+6 in the *Ritual of Abduction* as a vertical (see also Ex. 79). As noted in the discussion of that music, 6–15 relates directly to 5–16, one of the fundamental harmonies, as a subset. Indeed, it occurs as a prominent vertical in *Spring Rounds* at R54+4, when it is immediately followed by 5–16. The occurrence of 6–15 here, however, may be somewhat secondary or at least preparatory: The final sketch for this music (on Sketchbook p. 63) corresponds exactly to the full statement of the theme at R86, based on 6-Z17 (Ex. 59b). An engraving error is also likely (G incorrectly replacing F).

Ex. 59a. *Introduction to Part 2:* R85

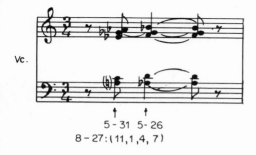

The section ends with a cadence and a codetta. The latter consists of a repeated phrase that echoes the Khorovod tune (horns) accompanied by the F-Gb dyad mentioned above (here E#-F#) played by strings. Here as elsewhere the cadence is of interest. As shown in Ex. 59a this consists of the succession 5-31/5-26, which sums to 8-27. Set 8-27 is a highly significant set in this movement, as has been suggested above in the comments on its complement, 4-27.

R86-R86+6

As indicated earlier, the section begins with 6-Z17 (Ex. 48). Set 6-Z43, the complement of 6-Z17, makes a brief appearance at R86+4, but its main role is reserved for the final movement. The other new events in this section are the ostinato figure based on 4-16 (Ex. 10) that begins in R86+3 and the accompanying trichords. (Since this material is developed in the next section and illustrated there, discussion will be postponed). The section ends with an arpeggiation of 4-27 leading to the new section.

Ex. 59b. Sketchbook p. 62

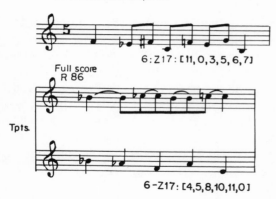

6:Z17: [11,0,3,5,6,7]

Full score
R 86

Tpts.

6-Z17: [4,5,8,10,11,0]

Sketchbook p. 62 contains an interesting sketch which shows that the theme at R86 was originally conceived as a single line (Ex. 59b). This justifies the reading of the configuration at R86 (if justification is required) as a combination of the trichord of trumpet 1 (3-1) and the tetrachord of trumpet 2 (4-12) forming 6-Z17.

Ex. 60. *Introduction to Part 2:* R87

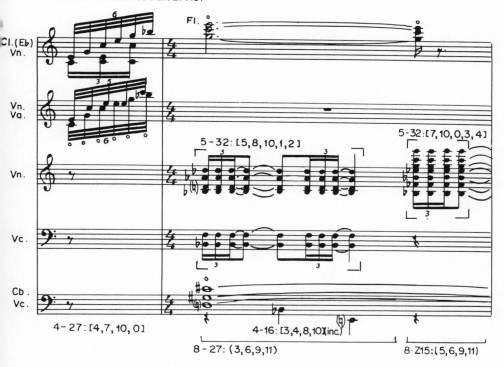

R87–R88+5

This is a beautifully composed section, with respect to both harmony and orchestration. Example 60 will suffice to indicate most of the main sets. (Here, as in most of the orchestral reductions, phrasing and articulation marks are omitted in the interest of economy.)

The large set, 8–27, holds over each of the first three beats of the measure. This set, as remarked above, is immediately preceded by a form of its complement, 4–27. On the last beat the large harmony changes to 8-Z15. Set 8-Z15 and set 8–27 are intervallically similar (R2) and share one 7-note subset, 7–32 (and hence are in the relation Rp). The latter relation is weakly represented since the two sets have in common only 6 notes. This common set 6-Z17: [0,1,2,4,7,8], however, is precisely the hexachord formed by the sustained flute and contrabass trichords in harmonics. The occurrence of 6-Z17 again, following its appearance at R86, indicates the extent to which this section is a development of the preceding music. This is even more evident in the first sketch of this passage (Sketchbook p. 62). There the initial harmony, excluding the ostinato bass figure, is 6-Z17: [3,4,5,7,10,11].

Perhaps the most prominent components of the passage, however, are the two forms of 5–32 (one of the basic harmonies in *The Rite of Spring*, it will be recalled): The two successive forms are transpositionally related ($t = 2$), producing one invariant, namely, the Bb that is the low note of the cello part and the first note of the ostinato figure (4–16).

R89–R89+3

The Khorovod tune returns (variant A, Ex. 57) with a simple trichord harmonization sounding against the trichord sustained by flutes from the previous section. Here the verticals formed are almost entirely without significance, either in the movement or in the work as a whole. It is possible that the individual lines of the setting are the most important elements: the upper two voices are both forms of 4–23, while the lower voice is 4–18.

R90–R90+3

This final section consists of a modified return of the music at R86 (Ex. 61a). The large sonority is 8–16, the complement of the ostinato figure introduced at R86+3 and continued in the development section that begins at R87.

Ex. 61a. *Introduction to Part 2:* R90

The final vertical in Ex. 61a and the final chord in the movement is 4–16 [6,7,11,1], the complement of 8–16. The cadential function of 4–16 has already been mentioned (Exx. 9, 106).

Ex. 61b. *Introduction to Part 2:* R90+3

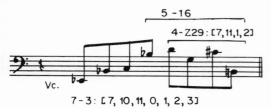

The cello solo at the end of the movement (Ex. 61b) is both enigmatic and anomalous because the set 7–3 has nothing to do with the music in the movement and is of little consequence in the work as a whole. The original idea appears on Sketchbook p. 50 (right margin), where the cello solo is given as Eb-Bb-G-A. This tetrachord is 4-Z29, the same set-type as the final tetrachord of the cello solo at R90+3. The sketch on p. 65 of the Sketchbook is even more revealing (Ex. 61c).[40] There the cello solo enters at what would become R90+2. And the equivalent of R90+3 contains on the last two beats a repetition of the tetrachord 4-Z29 (D-G-C#-B), the final tetrachord of 7–3. This emphasizes the importance of 4-Z29, a fundamental set in the subsequent movement, within the set 7–3.

An additional feature of the sketch (Ex. 61c) was not retained in the final version. This is the vertical 4-23 (B-C#-E-F#) brought in on the last beat of the measure by cellos and contrabasses in harmonics. The set is

40. Omitted from Ex. 61c for typographical reasons are the following orchestrational notes for the string harmonics on the last beat (4-23): 4 CB Soli senza sord./ (sans harm. 2 Celli Soli/2 Celli Soli sul do accorder en si grave./senza sord.

Ex. 61c. Sketchbook p. 65

of the same type as the set that underlies the Khorovod tune at the beginning of the next movement.

Mystic Circle of the Adolescents (R91)

R91–R92+3

This opening section features the first full harmonization of variant A of the Khorovod tune presented in the *Introduction to Part 2* (Ex. 57), with an extension. The Sketchbook (p. 55) informs us that the harmonization originally was to have been trichordal, virtually identical to a transposition of the passage at R89 in the *Introduction,* with set 4–8 in the accompanying parts (as at R101). The final version, however, is far more elaborate and structured: each upper voice note, almost without exception, has one or two fixed harmonies and most of these verticals are significant sets in the work as a whole (Ex. 62).[41] Some comments on these sets follow.

Set 5–31 at R91+1 (Ex. 62) is, of course, one of the basic harmonies in *The Rite of Spring,* as remarked several times before. Here it serves a cadential function. The two forms are transpositionally related, with $t = 9$, a level that produces maximum invariance, the invariant subset being 4–28 (which is not an explicit set in this passage). The other cadential harmony is 4–Z29 at R92+2, a set that occurs within the passage as well, harmonizing F#, together with 4–17. The latter is one of the earliest atonal sets (see n. 7).

Its strongest relation here is to 5–16 and 5–32, of which it is a subset. Set 4–12, which harmonizes E and C#, is very familiar to the reader at this point, and 5–16 and 5–32, again, are basic to *The Rite of Spring.* Set 6–Z13[42] appears here for the first time in the work (replacing 4–17 as harmony for F#), and, like 4–17, its structural role here can be explained in terms of its relation to 5–16 and 5–31; both are subsets of 6–Z13. Two sets, 4–14 and 5–27, neither relate well at all to the other sets in the passage, nor are they significant sets elsewhere in the music. Furthermore, set 5–27 provides an exception to the generalization that metrically accented harmonies are significant.

41. Example 62 excludes the ostinato figure 4–23 in cello and contrabass. This set is identical with respect to pc to the first phrase of the tune.
42. See also Ex. 77. Examples 89 and 103 display the complement of 6–Z13 (6–Z42).

Ex. 62. *Mystic Circle of the Adolescents:* R91

R93–R96+3

This section is so highly contrapuntal that the harmonic component seems to be minimal: that is, that the harmonies formed would be more or less arbitrary with respect to the movement and to the work as a whole. This is the case, to some extent, but on the other hand there is a considerable amount of regularity. The main components are melodic lines formed from 4–10 (Ex. 63a), 5–23 (Ex. 63b), and 4–23 (Ex. 63c), accompanied by major seconds (or ninths) in an ostinato pattern that forms a chromatic set (e.g., 5–1 in Ex. 63a). (It is possible that these seconds derive from the Khorovod tune).

The sketches (Sketchbook pp. 51, 55–58) do not illuminate the section, for they resemble the final version closely, with the differences in pitch level and instrumentation that one encounters often in the Sketchbook.

As indicated in Ex. 63, however, significant sets are formed. Notice in particular that 4-Z15 and 4–16 support the end-notes of the tune in Ex. 63b. In the same example, 4–11 (the major tetrachord) is maximally similar to 4–10 (the minor tetrachord), and 6-Z49 is a set that occurs in the *Sacrificial Dance*, together with its complement 6-Z28 (Exx. 88a, 97). The only anomaly is 5–15; this is its only appearance in the entire composition. However, it relates locally to 4–16, one of its three 4-note subsets.

Example 63c is representative of the final passage in the section: 4–23 (two forms) is counterpointed against 4–10, and the pattern of accompanying seconds (here ninths) continues. (In fact, all three linear components are ostinato, as can be ascertained from the complete score.) Even in this more complicated situation, where the harmonies are clearly secondary, the sets formed are of interest. All occur elsewhere in the work, although none are especially prominent. However, sets 5–19 and 5–28[43] have connections to more important hexachords (6–30 and 6-Z17/43) and tetrachords (4-Z15 and 4-Z29, in particular), so that they are not completely detached from more fundamental harmonies. Both reappear in the next section.

43. The most prominent previous occurrence of 5–28 is at R86+3.

Ex. 63a. *Mystic Circle of the Adolescents:* R93+1

Ex. 63b. *Mystic Circle of the Adolescents:* R94

Ex. 63c. *Mystic Circle of the Adolescents:* R95

R97–R98+1

The seconds feature of the previous section is continued in this section
in the form of the fixed dyad, C#-D#, expressed first as a ninth (Ex. 64)
then as a trilled second (Ex. 65). Further, Eb is sustained by horns up to
R98.[44] This stationary feature of course affects the harmonies, as did the
chromatic seconds in the previous section.

The main melodic element in the section, as shown in Ex. 64, is based
upon set 5-28, a harmony in the previous section. (Among the relations
of 5-28 to more important harmonies mentioned there, the relation to
6-30 seems to be the most explicit one here; the latter set is formed by
the upper voice combined with the sustained Eb in horns [0,2,3,6,8,9].)
The fifth in the melody suggests an association with the fourths in 4-10
at R93+4 and 5-23 at R94, and this association is strengthened by the
inversion of the fifth in the following passage (Ex. 65). Of the remaining
harmonies in Ex. 64, 4-5 is relatively significant in the movement (See
Exx. 68, 70) and 7-19 is the complement of 5-19, which was discussed
in connection with the previous section (Ex. 63c). Once again, as in the
previous section (Ex. 63b), the two harmonies 4-16 and 4-Z15 are in a
terminal position.

Example 65, from the Sketchbook, shows the first part of a pencil
sketch that corresponds almost exactly to the music at R98. Since the
trilled C#-D# is a fixed feature here, the harmonies with and without it
are indicated below the example. Of these, three will be unfamiliar to the
reader and are relatively insignificant in the work as a whole. Sets 5-6
(see Exx. 3a, 3c) and 5-9 (Exx. 13, 57) both contain 4-Z15, which somewhat justifies their appearance here, while set 4-7 is associated with 4-18
as in Ex. 44. Pc set 6-31, one of the hexachords of 7-32, occurs for the
first time. Only one set, 4-18, is unchanged by the trill. This set, so characteristic of *The Rite of Spring,* is formed precisely when the upper voice
changes from D to D# on the fifth quarter note.

---

44. As noted earlier, the function of such emphasized individual pc's is beyond
the scope of this study. But the association with Eb-Db of the *Augurs of Spring* chord
is quite obvious here.

Ex. 64. *Mystic Circle of the Adolescents:* R97+2

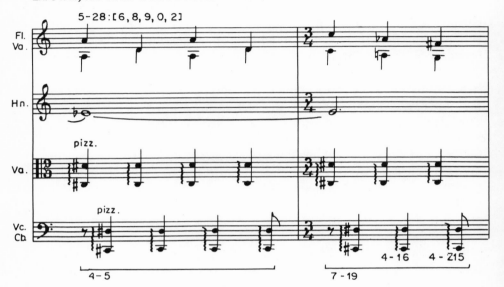

Ex. 65. Sketchbook p. 54

without trill: 4 - Z15   5 - 6   4 - Z15   4 - 7   5 - 32
with trill: 5 - 9   7 - Z18   5 - 9   6 - 31   (4 - 18)   7 - 16

R99–R103+1

With regard to harmony, this final section is much more regulated than the previous two sections. This is evident in the harmonization of the Khorovod tune at the beginning of the section. Example 66a shows this harmonization of the tune, the only occurrence of variant C in Ex. 57, which is based on set 4–10.[45] (Incidentally, 4–10 is in the set-complex relation K to all the hexachords in this section.) The set names below the staff indicate the minute changes, either in the melody or in one of the supporting voices. The set names above the staff indicate the changes over a 3/2 grouping of the notes of the tune.

With the exception of 4–4 and 4–9, all the tetrachords shown in Ex. 66a are important in the work and will be familiar from the preceding discussion. (The complement of 4–13 is prominent in *Augurs of Spring* at R31 and 4–13 occurs elsewhere in the work.) As the sketches will indicate (Exx. 66c–66e), the original ideas for the harmonization did not include the rhythmic displacements in tenor and bass. In Ex. 66b (by the author, not by Stravinsky) these displacements are eliminated; as a result, 4–4, 4–9, and 4–17 disappear, 4-Z15 is replaced by 4–25 on the third beat of the first measure, and 4-Z29 replaces 4–17 on the third beat of the second measure. In light of this rhythmic reinterpretation, therefore, sets 4–4 and 4–9, the unfamiliar sets, may be regarded as the result of a rhythmic feature; they arise in a way that is analogous to the suspension in traditional tonal music; i.e., they are not fundamental to the setting.

In relation to the more basic harmonies of *The Rite of Spring*, all the tetrachords (excluding 4–4 and 4–9) of Ex. 66a are significant. For instance, with one exception all are subsets of at least one of the sets 5–16, 5–31, and 5–32, and remarkably enough, 4–18 is a subset of all of these. The exception, of course, is the whole-tone tetrachord, 4–25. Moreover, 4–25 is maximally dissimilar to 4-Z15, which it replaces as harmonization of B at the beginning of the second measure. This strong contrast does not occur in the sketches. (4–25 is also maximally dissimilar to 4–13 and 4–18.) However, maximum intervallic similarity holds between many of the tetrachordal pairs.

Of the larger sets indicated at the top of Ex. 66a, all of which relate to more basic harmonies in the work, 6-Z23 deserves special attention, for it is the set that begins the next movement, *Honoring of the Chosen One.*

---

45. At one point, late in the composing of the *Introduction*, Stravinsky used variant C in the opening music, at about R82 (see Sketchbook p. 105, third entry).

Ex. 66a. *Mystic Circle of the Adolescents:* R99

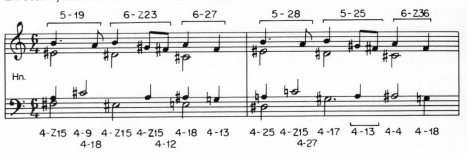

4-Z15 4-9 4-Z15 4-Z15 4-18 4-13   4-25 4-Z15 4-17 4-13 4-4 4-18
       4-18   4-12   4-27

Ex. 66b

4-Z15 4-18 4-25 4-12 4-18 4-13   4-25 4-27 4-Z29 4-13 4-12 4-18
             4-Z15

The amount of effort Stravinsky expended before he arrived at the final harmonization (Ex. 66a) is suggested by the sketches for the passage (Exx. 66c–66e).[46] The first sketch (Ex. 66c) appears alone on p. 46. In both this and the following sketch the tune stands at the distance of a tritone from the final version, a discrepancy that will not be discussed here, since it probably has to do with linear components of longer range— excluded from the present study. The trichordal harmonization is obviously quite primitive compared with the final version, although some features of the final version are present, most noticeably the set 5-19 shown in Ex. 66a (see also 7-19 in Ex. 64). Set 6-31, which does not play a role in the final version, is nevertheless closely related to one of the fundamental harmonies, 7-32, as remarked in connection with Ex. 65.

Example 66d, the next sketch, retains the pitch level and the 3/4 meter of the first sketch but introduces the tetrachords, all of which occur in the final version except 4-23, 4-28, and 4-Z29. Sets 4-Z15 and 4-18 are interchanged with reference to the final version; it will be recalled that the two are often closely associated in *The Rite of Spring* (Exx. 3c, 31).

The sketch in Ex. 66e occurs on the same page as one that corresponds almost exactly to Ex. 66d, except that it is transposed to the final pitch level.[47] This sketch (Ex. 66e) features 4-16, also an important tetrachord in the work. With regard to rhythm and the motion of the individual lines (especially the tenor) it represents a return to the simpler conception of Ex. 66c.

The remainder of *Mystic Circle of the Adolescents* includes several features of particular interest. First, varient A of the Khorovod tune returns at R100 but with a harmonization that differs from that at R91.[48] This is followed by a restatement of the tune (and harmonization) as at R91, closing with the cadential succession shown in Ex. 67a; this consists of 4-14 and 4-Z29, which sum to the diatonic set 6-33.

46. Not all the sketches are shown here. The sketch at the top of Sketchbook p. 53 is almost identical to Ex. 66d but transposed by a tritone, the sketch on Sketchbook p. 62 is almost the same as the final version, and the sketch on p. 64 is identical to it.

47. The assumption that the position of the sketches on the Sketchbook page corresponds to chronology may not always be correct. Here the sketch in the middle of p. 53 (Ex. 66e) might well have preceded the sketch at the top (not shown). Robert Craft's assumption ("Commentary to the Sketches," p. 4, accompanying *The Rite of Spring: Sketches 1911–1913*) of a simple positional correspondence to chronology can be disputed with convincing evidence in the Sketchbook.

48. So much space has been devoted to the treatment of variant C at R99 that the harmonization of variant A at this point will be passed over. Suffice it to point out that it ends with set 7-31, one of the basic harmonies.

Ex. 66c. Sketchbook p. 46

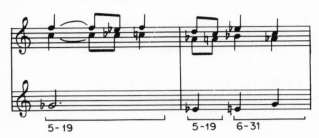

                    5-19   5-19   6-31

Ex. 66d. Sketchbook p. 50

4-Z15 4-23 4-18   4-18 4-Z15 4-17   4-17 4-Z15 4-Z29   4-Z15 4-18 (3-4)
      (3-7)   4-17   4-12   4-28

Ex. 66e. Sketchbook p. 53

4 Cor.

    4-16   4-27 4-18   4-17 4-18   4-18   4-16

Ex. 67a. *Mystic Circle of the Adolescents:* R100+4

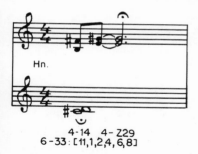

4-14   4- Z29
6 -33 : [11,1,2,4, 6,8]

Set 4–14 was included in the harmonization of the Khorovod tune at R91
(Ex. 62), and 4-Z29 is familiar to the reader at this juncture in a number
of contexts. This cadence is transposed at R101+4 (Ex. 67b), with $t = 7$;
the resulting invariant subset is 4–23, the set that is the basis of variant
A of the Khorovod tune.

Ex. 67b. *Mystic Circle of the Adolescents:* R101+4

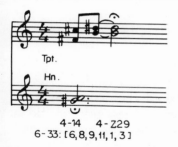

4-14   4- Z29
6- 33: [6,8,9,11,1, 3]

The hexachord 6–33 here, as well as the invariant subset, clearly refers
sonically to the two variants of the Khorovòd tune that occur in the section. (With respect to upper voice and rhythm, this cadence resembles
the one at R85 [Ex. 59a].)

The cadential succession is reiterated at R102–R102+2, with the per-
formance instruction *poco a poco accelerando*. That passage ends in a
remarkable way, with a melodic statement of 8–16 that sounds against
a notated glissando without harmonic significance (Ex. 68). (It will be
recalled that the complement of 8–16 [4–16] has a closing function elsewhere in the music [e.g., Ex. 9].)

Ex. 68. *Mystic Circle of the Adolescents:* R103

Moreover, this final passage ends with the vertical 4-Z15, another closing harmony, which in this context is associated with its Z-correspondent, 4-Z29. There follows the famous 11/4 measure, in which the hexachord 6-Z23 is introduced in preparation for the following movement (Ex. 69).

Ex. 69. *Mystic Circle of the Adolescents:* R103+1

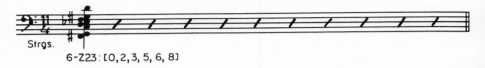

Honoring of the Chosen One (R104)

R104-R110+3

The opening music, shown in Ex. 70, comprises three sets: 4-5, 6-Z23, and 7-Z36. This is the second appearance of 6-Z23, the first being at the end of the previous movement (Ex. 69). The two sets are transpositionally related ($t = 1$), with two invariants, pc's 3 and 6: the prominent D# and F# in the upper voice of the second form at R104. Although 6-Z23 is a new set in the music, it has a number of connections with the material in the preceding movement. In particular, it contains both 4-Z15 and 4-Z29 (twice) and thus links up to the end of the *Mystic Circle,* where those sets are in the forefront. More important are its connections to the fundamental harmonies of the work as a whole: it is a subset of 8-18, and perhaps more significant, it is one of the six hexachords of 7-31.

The large set, 7-Z36 (Ex. 70), is the complement of the set that underlies the main theme of the *Procession of the Sage,* a theme introduced in the *Ritual of Two Rival Tribes* (Ex. 41b). There is, however, no explicit association of the two sets. Set 7-Z36 is one of the eight 7-note subsets of 8-18, which also include the fundamental harmonies 7-16, 7-31, and 7-32. Indeed, if B# in the embellishing flute slide in Ex. 70 is included

Ex. 70. *Honoring of the Chosen One:* R104

4-5:[7,8,9,1]   6-Z23:[1,3,4,6,7,9]
7-Z36: [1,3,4,6,7,8,9]

in the reading of the opening passage, the total set is 8–18: (10,11,2,5), as shown in Ex. 5.[49]

The set 4–5 (Ex. 70) has a local association with the form of this set that occurs at the end of the melodically stated 8–16 at R103 in *Mystic Circle of the Adolescents* (Ex. 68). However, it is not important in any of the other movements and does not relate strongly to any of the fundamental harmonies, although it is a subset of 7–16. Like 4–3 in the upper voice of Ex. 70 the scope of its relations does not extend beyond the immediate context.

At R106 the last 7 notes of the 8–16 figure shown in Ex. 68 are stated by trumpets, and the last note (D#), on the downbeat of R106+1, is within the vertical 4-Z15: [1,3,6,7], thus verifying the association of 6-Z23 and the tetrachord that was pointed out above.[50] This is followed immediately by a return of 6-Z23 in the form in which it occurred at R103+1 (Ex. 69).

A permutation of the 8–16 melodic figure (Ex. 68) is introduced at R107 and leads to a repetition of 4-Z15 and 6-Z23, as described in the paragraph just above. Analysis of the substructure of 8–16 either in its original form or in the changed order as here does not reveal any subtleties that clarify the purpose of the set in this movement. For example, it does not contain 7-Z36, 6-Z23, or the complement of the latter and thus has no direct harmonic association with these prominent sets.

At R109 new sets are introduced over the pedal bass A (Ex. 71) and at R109+2 the succession is continued, this time to include 4-Z29 (not shown in Ex. 71); thus, the complete list of sets is 4–13, 4-Z15, 4–18, and 4-Z29. All except 4-Z29 are tetrachords in the harmonization of the Khorovod tune in the preceding movement at R99 (Ex. 66a); the reference is unequivocal.[51]

R111–R116+2
The fixed pitch F, with embellishing "neighbor" notes (Ex. 72) and the trichord 3–5 (at R112+3 and in similar passages [Ex. 73]) are prominent

49. The first sketch for this opening, on Sketchbook p. 59, contains no initial embellishment of the first chord. The matter of 8–18 as an explicit harmony here becomes even more problematic at R105+2, where the duet score gives B# as part of the chord, whereas the full score at that point is identical to R104.

50. At R106 the duet score and the sketch (Sketchbook p. 67) give the first 3 notes of the trumpet figure as A#-G-B. In the full score the order is B-G-A#. Obviously the set remains the same in both cases.

51. The upper 3 notes of each vertical in Ex. 71 form the trichord 3–5, a prominent set in this movement altogether but excluded from the discussion, along with other trichords, as stated earlier.

Ex. 71. *Honoring of the Chosen One:* R109

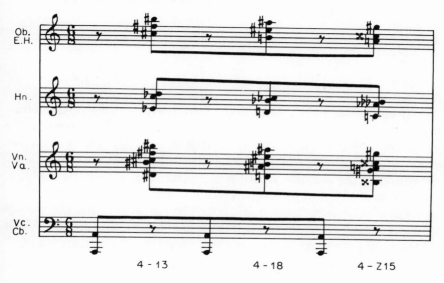

features of this section that will not be taken into consideration in the following account of its harmonic content.[52]

Ex. 72. *Honoring of the Chosen One:* R111+1

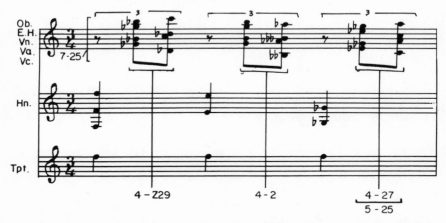

The passage shown in Ex. 72 is difficult to interpret. Two of the tetrachords formed in the upper register, 4-Z29 and 4-27, are important in the work; the third, 4-2, is anomalous in this regard. And the sonorities formed on each beat, including the brass parts, are not significant elsewhere, with the exception of the last one, which is 5-25 (Ex. 32). This is the complement of the sum of the upper parts, 7-25, and both sets relate directly to the fundamental hexachord, 6-27. It can be concluded that the passage is not highly structured from the harmonic standpoint. The melodic wholetone tetrachord in the upper voice is obvious and requires no comment.

---

52. The motive in brass here resembles that at the opening of *Ritual of Two Rival Tribes,* R5, but the context of course, is entirely different.

Ex. 73. *Honoring of the Chosen One:* R112+3

The new passage introduced at R112+3 brings in four sets: 4–8, 5–6, 5–7, and 5–Z18 (Ex. 73). Of these, 4–8 is the most familiar, having occurred previously in prominent situations (Exx. 20a, 20b). Set 5–Z18 is less familiar, but it is not an uncommon set in the work. It is formed in *Kiss of the Earth* at R71 and its complement occurs in the *Introduction to Part 2* at R90 (Ex. 61a, lower staff). Set 5–7 is one of the main sets in the *Sacrificial Dance* at R174 (Ex. 98), while the remaining set, 5–6, is not particularly consequential elsewhere in the work (Ex. 3a).

Ex. 74. *Honoring of the Chosen One:* R116+2

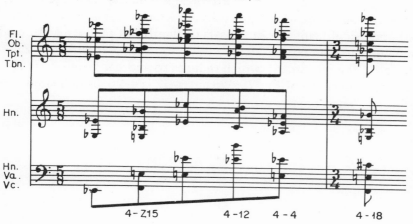

A number of the verticals formed in the extension of the passage shown in Ex. 73 that begins at R114 do not relate closely to the fundamental harmonies and are not presented elsewhere in any important capacity (e.g.,

5-11, 5-5). Thus, this portion of the movement is not highly regulated
harmonically, compared with many others in *The Rite of Spring*. The
condition changes at the climax of the section at R116+2 (Ex. 74) with
the appearance of the familiar sets 4-Z15 and 4-12 (and the anomalous
4-4) and the close on the cadential set 4-18.[53] The upper voice is 4-22:
[8,10,0,3], a diatonic formation.

R117-R120+3
This final section of the movement is essentially the same as the first
section, R104-R110+3. One curious aspect of the beginning of the section
is the partial repetition of the figure based on 8-16 (Ex. 68) first stated in
the *Mystic Circle of the Adolescents:* The second note of the figure should
be G according to previous occurrences (e.g., at R108+1). In the full score,
but not in the duet, it is given as E. The set formed with E is 5-7 (cf. Ex.
98).

Evocation of the Ancestors (R121)

R121-R128 (all [no sections])
The main harmonic content of this short movement is summarized in its
opening music (Ex. 75), which begins with a fragment of the upper voice
of the previous movement here transferred to the low register of the or-
chestra.[54] This is another of those extraordinary musical statements, perhaps more typical of the later Stravinsky, in which diverse components,
all based upon significant sets or subsets of significant sets, are combined
in a seemingly simple texture. Most familiar to the reader will be 6-27
at the onset of the movement, which reduces to another familiar set, 5-
32, in the third measure of Ex. 75. Within 5-32 is 4-26, as indicated.

53. In the duet score this closing sonority is 3-5. The cello C♯ is not represented.
54. Cf. *StrAM,* Ex. 79, and accompanying comments on the Sketchbook.

Ex. 75. *Evocation of the Ancestors:* R121+1

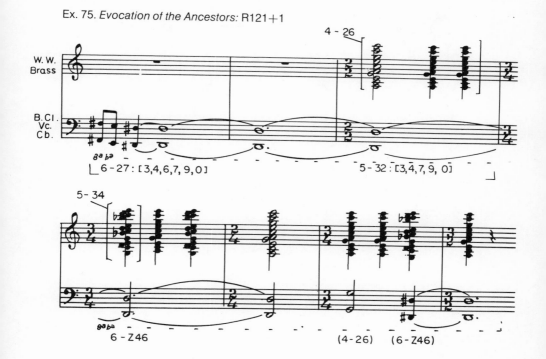

Ex. 76a. *Ritual of the Ancestors:* R130

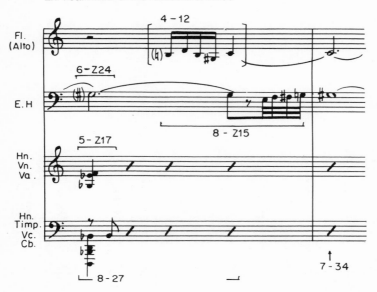

Ex. 76b. *Ritual of the Ancestors:* R130+5

When the upper parts change to 5–34, this harmony combines with the sustained D# in the bass to form 6-Z46, a set that makes its first and only prominent appearance here, but whose complement, 6-Z24, is consequential with respect to the harmony of the next movement (Ex. 76a). Set 6-Z46 contains 5–32, which is not a compositionally distinct component here. (It is the 5-note subset of the vertical, excluding D.) Another important subset relation here involves 5–34: This set contains 4–27 twice, a relation that gains significance in view of the fact that the large set formed by the passage is 8–27 (cf. Ex. 60).

There is yet another statement of 5–32 in the course of the movement: on the first beat of R126+2 (not shown), where the upper voice changes from the reiterated C-D succession to bring in Eb. This forms 5–32: [7, 10,0,3,4], which is the transposed inversion of the form shown in Ex. 75 ($t = 7$). The result is maximum invariance, with four pc's held in common between the two forms.

The movement ends with 5–32 (as in Ex. 75) followed by a momentary statement of 4-Z29: [9,10,0,4], as the bass changes to Bb in preparation for the forthcoming movement. The final transition to the next movement is made by bassoons, each line forming a set. The most significant of these is 8–18: (7,10,1,2) played by third bassoon and contrabasson (see Sketchbook p. 75).

Ritual of the Ancestors (R129)

R129-R134+3

The opening music of the movement involves only a small number of sets, most of which are shown in Ex. 76a. At the beginning 5-Z17 is gradually constructed, attaining the form shown in Ex. 76a at R129+2. Although this set occurs elsewhere in the work (as does its Z-correspondent, 5-Z37), it is prominent only here. Set 5-Z17 is probably more correctly regarded as a subset of the two hexachords in the section, 6-Z24, with G# in English horn, and 6-Z19, which is formed when the final note of the flute changes from C to Cb at R130+6 (Ex. 76b).

Set 6-Z24 (Ex. 76a) is most interesting in this context because it is the complement of 6-Z46 in the previous movement (Ex. 75)—thus preserving interval content and linking the two sections harmonically. Set 6-Z19 (Ex. 76b) occurs in the opening of the *Introduction to Part 2* (Ex. 54) and is an important set in the first and second sections of the *Sacrificial Dance*. Both 6-Z24 and 6-Z19 are subsets of the fundamental set 7–32.

The melodically stated set 4–12 is the predominant figure played by flute. This, of course, is a very familiar set with a number of associations in the other movements (Exx. 11, 12, 23, 43, 47, 62, 74). The transformation of 4–12 at R130+5 (Ex. 76b) is interesting because of the invariants with respect to the form in Ex. 76a: D, B (Cb), and Ab (G#): three invariants are possible only under inversion and for only one value of *t* (here 10).

Sets larger than the hexachord are also of significance in this opening music: the 8-note sets 8-Z15 and 8-27 and the 7-note set 7–34, which occurs elsewhere. The latter set relates to the more fundamental harmonies 7–31 and 7–32 through the common subsets 6-Z23 and 6-Z24.

Ex. 77. *Ritual of the Ancestors:* R131

At R131 a new melody is introduced by alto flute; the first part consists of set 4–10, the second of 5–10 (Ex. 77). Both sets are of course familiar (e.g., Exx. 8, 53). In this movement, 5–10 relates to 6-Z24, of which it is a subset, along with 5-Z17. The hexachord formed by this passage, 6-Z13, is perhaps of secondary importance. It is, however, a subset of the fundamental harmony 7–31 and thus relates to a larger harmonic scheme.[55] This relation becomes explicit in the next passage.

Ex. 78. *Ritual of the Ancestors:* R132

The main theme of the movement, also based on 4–10, enters at R132 (Ex. 78) against the already established melody discussed immediately above. As a result, one new pc is introduced, pc8 (the G# in the theme), forming the 7-note set 7–31: [8,10,11,1,2,4,5]. Since no new pitch

---

55. The complement of 6-Z13 (6-Z42) replaces 6-Z28 as the opening chord of the *Sacrificial Dance* in the 1943 revision of that movement.

classes are introduced until R133+3, this fundamental harmony directly governs this portion of the movement. This is not the only occurrence of 7-31 in the movement. It is formed on the first beat of R134 and again on the first beat of R134+1. The three nonidentical forms of 7-31 are related operationally in such a way that maximum invariance holds between any two forms: six pc's are held fixed. All the hexachords that result are significant in the work but are not distinct compositional components in the context of any of the forms of 7-31: 6-Z23, 6-Z13, and 6-27.

Ex. 79. *Ritual of the Ancestors:* R133+3

Following the long passage based on 7-31, the 3-note motive from the *Introduction to Part 2* (Ex. 58) is brought in against 5-10 and its accompaniment (Ex. 79). The purpose of this is not clear; perhaps it has to do with the choreography, although there is no evidence of this in the description of the Stravinsky–Nijinsky choreography for this movement.[56] Set 6-15 relates to 7-16 in the larger harmonic scheme, but it occurs here in the context of 7-Z38 (cf. Ex. 58).

Ex. 80. *Ritual of the Ancestors:* R134

At R134 begins the final passage of the section. Here a new set is introduced as a countermelody to the main theme shown in Ex. 78, 6-Z25 (Ex. 80). This hexachord is one of the seven hexachords of 7-32 and has a basic role in the *Sacrificial Dance* at R151+1. The ordering of the hexachords is motivic, of course: the three successive descending fourths refer to the boundary interval of the main theme (Ex. 78).

R135-R137+5
This section serves as a contrasting passage between the two tutti sections that carry the main theme of the movement. It introduces a new set, 4-

56. See Appendix III to *The Rite of Spring* Sketchbook. A description of Stravinsky's concept of the choreography is recorded in a copy of the duet score.

Ex. 81. *Ritual of the Ancestors:* R135

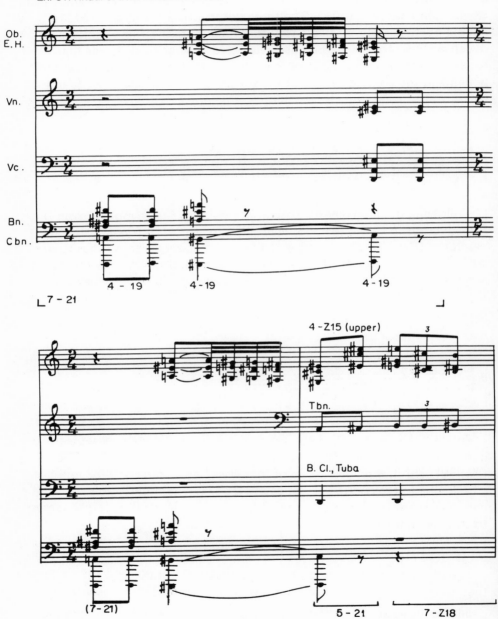

19—its first occurrence in the work—which is the predominant harmony
in the section. The three successive forms of 4-19 are shown in Ex. 81.
The second is a transposition of the first ($t = 11$) and the third is an inversion of the second ($t = 10$). Set 4-19 is contained within 6-Z24 and 5-Z17,
both prominent sets in the opening music of the movement (Ex. 76a).
The relation to 5-Z17, however, is probably the more immediate one, as
indicated by Sketchbook p. 78 (Ex. 82), the first sketch of this passage,
where two forms of 4-19 are given and then immediately repeated with
an additional note for each, forming 5-Z17.

Ex. 82. Sketchbook p. 78

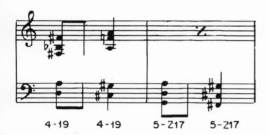

Large sets are formed, in this section as well, as indicated in Ex. 81.
Set 7-21 is the sum of the three forms of 4-19 (excluding the embellishing
chromatic motion in the upper parts), and it is followed by its complement in the third measure of Ex. 81. The most significant previous occurrence of the latter is in the *Introduction to Part 2* at R81+1 (Ex. 55). The
other 7-note set in Ex. 81, 7-Z18, is represented by its complement in
other movements—for example, in *Kiss of the Earth* at R71 (Ex. 12) and
in *Honoring of the Chosen One* at R112+3 (Ex. 73). Set 7-Z18 is a subset
of the more fundamental harmony 8-18.[57]
Beginning at R136 the music at R135 shown in Ex. 81 is transposed.
This is not the only change, however. A new configuration is introduced,
the upper voice of which derives motivically from the chromatic figure
played by trombone in R135+2 (Ex. 81). This added component brings
in new harmonies, the most important of which are 4-18 (its first occurrence in this movement) and two of the other basic harmonies, 5-31 and
5-32.[58] Note, in particular, that 4-18 once again has a cadential function

57. The original sketch for m. 3 of Ex. 81 differs markedly from the final version
(see Sketchbook p. 79). The 7-note set formed there is 7-Z36, another of the 7-note
subsets of 8-18.
58. The duet score differs from the full score in the measures shown here as Ex. 83a
in that in the latter the horn sustains a (sounding) F throughout. Without the F the

Ex. 83a. *Ritual of the Ancestors:* R136+3

4-19   4-11   5-31 5-21

Ex. 83b. *Ritual of the Ancestors:* R137+2

4-19   4-14   5-31 5-21

Ex. 83c. *Ritual of the Ancestors:* R137+5

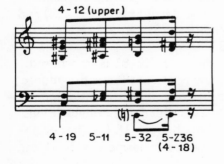

4-19   5-11   5-32 5-Z36
                          (4-18)

(Ex. 83c). Here, as in a number of other locations in *The Rite of Spring*, it appears that the linear component is controlled to a large extent by the verticals.[59] Nevertheless, the development of the upper voice is of interest: Whereas the sets formed in Exx. 83a and 83b are relatively trivial, the last one (Ex. 83c) is 4–12, which relates to the earlier music of the movement (Exx. 76a, 76b).

R138–R138+5

In this short tutti section, which may be regarded as the climax of the movement, the main theme is stated for the last time, at its original pitch level but in a different setting.

Ex. 84. *Ritual of the Ancestors:* R138

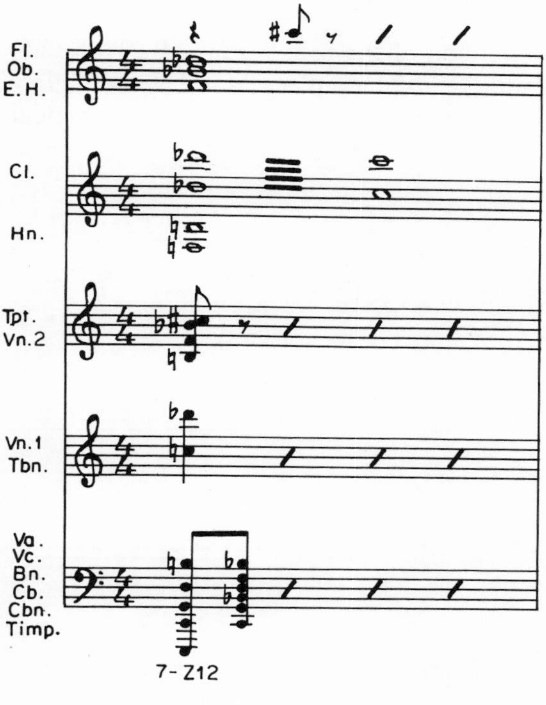

7- Z12

---

last two verticals are 4–18 and 4–19. Furthermore, in the duet score of R137+5 (Ex. 83c) the bass E does not continue at the bottom of the final vertical, making the set 4–18—the common cadential harmony in the work.

59. There is a sketch only for the first of the passages shown in Ex. 83 (Sketchbook p. 80).

As indicated in Ex. 84, this setting expresses the large set 7-Z12. And whenever pc4 is added to the accompanying sonority as a result of the trilled ostinato figure played by clarinets and violins beginning in R138+1 (not shown), the total harmony is 8–13. Neither 7-Z12 nor 5-Z12 is important elsewhere in the music.[60] Set 7-Z12 is connected, however, to the more fundamental harmony 7–31 in the following way: Both are subsets of 8–13 and both contain 6-Z49—indeed, it is the only hexachord common to both—and 6-Z49, although not an explicit subset of the harmony here (Ex. 84), is especially significant as a "background" event because it is the complement of the first chord in the next movement (*Sacrificial Dance*), 6-Z28. Set 6-Z49 is significant elsewhere as well (Exx. 51, 63b).

R139–R141+4

This final section is a modified version of the first section, R129–R134+3. The modifications are significant. Set 4-Z15 replaces 4–12 as the melodic figure at R139+5 and the identical set is given momentarily as a vertical (Ex. 85).

Ex. 85. *Ritual of the Ancestors:* R139+5

                                                                              (4 – 3)

---

60. As noted earlier, however, the Z-correspondent of 5-Z12 (5-Z36) is the basis of the main theme in *Ritual of Two Rival Tribes* (Ex. 41b) (see also 5-Z12 in Ex. 41a).

At the same time the accompaniment figure is reduced to the dyad D-Bb and the melodic note Db is embellished by Cb, a reference to the first two notes of the main theme. The resulting set, 4-3, which is not a significant set in the work, is perhaps best explained as a combination of these fragments.

Beginning with R140+1 a series of rapid figurations is introduced, each of which embellishes the Db-Cb dyad in the melody. Although one might expect these figurations to recapitulate significant sets in the movement, this is not the case, with only one exception.

Ex. 86a. *Ritual of the Ancestors:* R140+1

Example 86a shows the set that arises from the first figuration: 4-7. This set occurs elsewhere (Exx. 44, 65) but is never prominent in the work. Of course, it has several connections (inclusion relations) to more important harmonies, 5-Z18, 6-Z19, and 6-Z43 being the most immediate relatives.

Ex. 86b. *Ritual of the Ancestors:* R140+3

Ex. 86c. *Ritual of the Ancestors:* R141+2

Example 86b, the exception mentioned above, shows the important set 4-12 as it is formed by the second embellishing figure (cf. Exx. 76a, 76b), and Ex. 86c shows 5-3, the most enigmatic set of the three. Set 5-3 has no significance in the work as a whole, and, indeed, this is its only prominent appearance (cf. Ex. 61b). It is possible that the trichord C-Eb-E replicates the trichord Bb-Db-D (3-3) formed by the accompanying dyad

and the upper voice Db, Ex. 85, but this ad hoc explanation is not especially convincing. Similarly, the final hexachord 6-5 (Ex. 86c) makes little
sense unless it is grouped with the preceding final statement of the motive
Db-Cb; this forms the 8-note set 8-16, which is, of course, one of the more
basic harmonies in the work.

The sketches for this final section (Sketchbook pp. 82-83) are illumi-
nating. With respect to the form of the work as a whole, it is astonishing
to learn that this movement was originally intended to be the last movement, following the *Sacrificial Dance.*[61] More relevant to the topic of this
study are two differences in detail between the sketches and the final
version. First, the accompaniment at R140 is not the dyad Bb-D but the
trichord A-Bb-D, which the melodic note Db creates the set 4-7: [9,10,1,
2]. The second difference is displayed in Ex. 87.

Ex. 87. Sketchbook p. 83

The set formed by the septolet here is 7-7: (7,8,0,1,2), the complement
of 5-7, which is the predominant set in the section beginning at R174
in the forthcoming movement. (The final D, of course, becomes the first
bass note in *Sacrificial Dance.*) Moreover, the correction involving the
deletion of the beam connection to C# as well as the staccato mark for
that C# more clearly associates the note with the following configuration
and justifies, to some extent, the reading of 8-16 as the main set of this
ending passage. The cadential function of 4-16 has been mentioned before
(Ex. 9), and 8-16 has a cadential function at the close of the *Mystic Circle
of the Adolescents* (Ex. 68).

Sacrificial Dance (R142)

R142-R148+2[62]

The final movement brings back a number of the harmonies that have
been stated in various ways in the preceding movements. At the same time

61. See Craft, "Commentary to the Sketches," p. 22.
62. An analysis of the first two sections of this movement, in terms of set-complex
theory, is given in *StrAM*, pp. 144-66. The reading of sets there is based on the 1943
revision; thus, some sets discussed there are omitted here. An additional difference

it introduces new harmonies or brings to the fore harmonies that had only minor roles in the other movements. The opening chord 6-Z28 is an example of the latter situation (Ex. 88a).[63]

Ex. 88a. *Sacrificial Dance:* R142

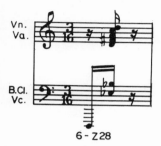

6 - Z28

This set is not prominent elsewhere in the work although it is present in a number of movements in a secondary role (Ex. 19). Its occurrence here in this primary role is not inconsequential with respect to fundamental harmonies, for it is one of the seven 6-note subsets of 7–32. Moreover, its complement, 6-Z49, which was mentioned in connection with the previous movement, is one of the six 6-note subsets of another fundamental harmony, 7–31.

Ex. 88b. Sketchbook p. 83

4 - 18   5-35 4 - 28

(Example 88b shows what may have been an initial idea for the opening of the *Sacrificial Dance,* in which the familiar tetrachord 4–18 is the principal set [a subset of 6-Z28 in the final version]. The identification is by no means certain, however, for this fragment can also be associated with

---

between the treatment here and the discussion in *StrAM* is that in the latter the sections were regarded as self-contained entities, whereas here it is possible to make specific references to the work as a whole. The significance of 7–31 and 7–32, especially, becomes evident.

63. With respect to changes of meter signature the full score differs from the duet score. Locations in the score always refer to the full score, not to the duet.

the sketch at the bottom of p. 84, a tentative sketch of the section that begins at R174.) Indeed, the extent to which the harmonies of this opening section relate to the fundamental 7-note sets 7–31 and 7–32 is quite remarkable, as will be demonstrated.

Ex. 89. *Sacrificial Dance:* R142+3

Example 89 shows the progression that follows the initial chord, 6-Z28. This involves two sets, 6–27 and 6-Z42. Set 6–27, of course, is familiar as one of the fundamental hexachords of the work; it is a subset of the basic 7-note sets 7–16, 7–31, and 7–32 (and contains the complements of those sets). Set 6-Z42 is not so familiar; its complement, 6-Z13, however, is formed at an important formal juncture in the *Ritual of the Ancestors* (Ex. 77). Set 6-Z42 contains 5–31 twice, as do 6–27 and 6-Z28. Thus, this common subset provides a specific linkage of the three sets.[64] Moreover, any two of the three sets are maximally similar with respect to interval content.[65]

Ex. 90. *Sacrificial Dance:* R144

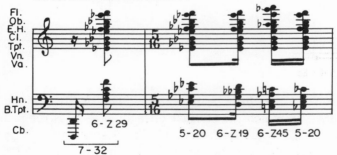

64. The common subset is explicit with respect to pc content only between 6-Z28 and 6-Z42. The pc intersection of these sets in the music is the important set 5–31: [6,9,0,2,3].

65. A complete summary of similarity relations among the hexachords in the *Sacrificial Dance* is given in *StrAM,* Ex. 147.

Thus far in the movement, none of the large harmonies has appeared. This changes at R144, as shown in Ex. 90, where 7–32 is formed. Within 7–32 is 6-Z29, a relatively new set in the music. Although both 6-Z29 and its complement, 6-Z50, have appeared in other movements, only 6-Z50 has been prominent (Exx. 21b, 47). Set 5–20, which follows 6-Z29, is a subset of 6-Z19, the next harmony in the progression and the set by which 5–20 relates (in a set-complex interpretation) to 7–32. Set 5–20 also relates to a number of other important sets, among them 6-Z43, 4–16, and 4-Z29. It is a superset of the latter in its only important appearance, in the *Introduction to Part 1* at R4, where it is formed by oboe D# against the accompanying sonority, 4-Z29 (see Ex. 13). Set 5–20 is also maximally similar (R1) to the more basic set 5–16.

The remaining harmony in the succession, 6-Z45, occurs only in this movement. However, its complement, 6-Z23, is familiar as the main hexachord in *Honoring of the Chosen One* (Ex. 69). Both relate to 5–31 and its complement.

Similarity relations among the three hexachords in the passage are interesting. Whereas 6-Z19 and 6-Z29 are maximally similar with respect to pc (sharing five pc's), and 6-Z29 and 6-Z45 are maximally similar with respect to interval content and maximally similar with respect to pc content (sharing set 5–31), the other two, 6-Z19 and 6-Z45, are maximally dissimilar with respect to interval content.

Ex. 91. *Sacrificial Dance:* R146

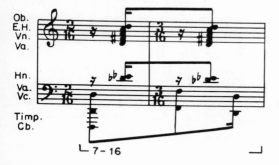

It was mentioned above that 6-Z42 (Ex. 89) is related by inclusion to 5–31, one of the fundamental harmonies (hence, its complement, 6-Z13, is a subset of 7–31). Set 6-Z42 is also related by inclusion to another of the basic harmonies, 7–16. This relation is stated explicitly at R146, where the change of bass figure brings in pc5, forming 7–16 in combination with 6-Z42 (Ex. 91). It will be recalled that 7–16 and 7–32 are maximally similar.)

Ex. 92. *Sacrificial Dance:* R148+1

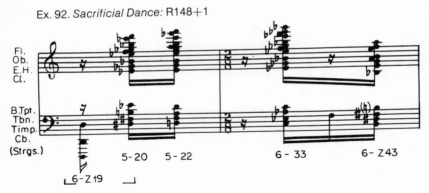

Example 92 shows the climactic passage that ends the first section of
the *Sacrificial Dance.* The first two sets are familiar, 6-Z19 and 5-20; in
this situation, however, 5-20 is more literally embedded in 6-Z19, the
latter being formed by the bass D and the chord, as shown. Set 5-22, which
follows, is also a subset of 6-Z19 and hence relates to 7-32. It is also a
subset of the complement of 6-Z19 (6-Z44) and hence relates to 7-16 as
well. (It will be recalled that 7-22, the complement of 5-22, is the enigmatic sonority at the end of the *Kiss of the Earth,* Ex. 49a. Its relation
to more fundamental sets is now clear.)

The third vertical in Ex. 92, set 6-33, does not fit neatly into the main
harmonic scheme of the work or movement but belongs to the diatonic
component. In this local context it merges with the following harmony
to form 8-13: (1,2,4,7), which, however, is not a significant set elsewhere
in the movement. It is of more than passing interest that Stravinsky changed
this chord to 6-Z45 in the 1943 revision.

Set 6-Z43, the last vertical in the progression, is not a familiar set (cf.
Ex. 30); its complement, 6-Z17, is, however.[66] It occurs in the *Introduction to Part 1* at R5, in *Ritual of the Rival Tribes* at R65+2 (as mentioned
previously), and, most importantly, at R86, as shown in Ex. 48. Although
6-Z43 does not relate directly to any of the fundamental 7-note sets, it
does relate to certain of the basic 8-note harmonies, notably 8-16 and
8-18.

R149-R166+4

The section begins with a radical change in texture, sonority, and rhythm.
The diatonic set 5-23 is introduced and reiterated in a setting involving
an alternation of 2/8 and 3/8 meter signatures. Subsequently a 3-note

66. In the duet score, the final vertical lacks pc10, making the set 5-28.

chromatic motive is introduced against this, producing the set 6-Z25 (Ex. 93a) at its termination.

Ex. 93a. *Sacrificial Dance:* R150+5

Linear statements of 5–23 were featured in Part 1, for example, in the *Introduction* at R3+1 (Ex. 7b), at R7+3 (bassoon), in *Augurs of Spring* (Ex. 22), and in Part 2 in *Mystic Circle of the Adolescents* at R94 (clarinet). Although 5–23 is most easily associated with the diatonic family of harmonies in *The Rite of Spring*, it relates to 7–32 through 6-Z25, which is explicitly presented here (Ex. 93a) as the chromatic motive ends on Bb. Set 6-Z25 is not especially prominent in the work, and only two instances have been cited (Exx. 56b, 80) thus far. It is, however, one of the seven hexachords of 7–32, six of which, altogether, occur in this section. Thus, although 7–32 never appears in the section, it is well represented by its hexachordal subsets.

The sketches for the section are in short score, for the most part, and are essentially the same as the final version. Yet there is one interesting and initially puzzling entry: the circled number *29,* which appears on Sketchbook pp. 92 and 93. It can be ascertained that there are exactly 29 pulses from the beginning of the section to the entry of the chromatic motive at R151. It seems likely that this temporal feature is what Stravinsky had in mind when he wrote down the mysterious prime number.[67]

---

67. Further investigation reveals other prime number relations in the movement. One is reminded of the prime number schemes devised by Ives in his sketches for the *Universe Symphony.*

Ex. 93b. Sketchbook p. 81

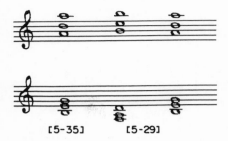

[5-35]   [5-29]

Relevant to the genesis of this music, in his comments on p. 81 of the Sketchbook, Craft (Craft, op. cit., p. 22) writes: "The Russian words identify the two entries in the upper right corner with the 'Sacrificial Dance'. The chords are related to the examples on the lower half of page 50, the center of page 51, and the next-to-top right of page 53." The chordal entry is reproduced in Ex. 93b, with the Russian words omitted. Although we can ignore, as most dubious, Craft's statement regarding the relation between these chords and the examples on pp. 50, 51, and 53, the relation between the chords and the section of the *Sacrificial Dance* that begins at R149 is quite interesting. As indicated in brackets in Ex. 93b, the two chords are 5-35 and 5-29. These, together with the set in the final version (Ex. 93a), 5-23, are subsets of the diatonic set, 7-35, and hence all four sets are related in a very basic and general way. Moreover, they are similar in the following respects: Both 5-29 and 5-35 are in the relations Rp and R2 to set 5-23. The Rp relation between the sketched chords and the set 5-23 in the final version is strongly represented: The common tetrachord between 5-35 and 5-23 is 4-23 and the common tetrachord between 5-29 and 5-23 is 4-14. Both tetrachords are prominent elsewhere in *The Rite of Spring,* of course. Here again we gain some insight into Stravinsky's way of associating harmonies.

Ex. 94. *Sacrificial Dance:* R155

At R154 the diatonic set 5–20 replaces 5–23 as the chord in the ostinato pattern (Ex. 94). It will be recalled that 5–20 occurred in the previous section, within 6-Z19 (Exx. 90, 92). The association of 5–20 with 5-
23 in the present context is not based on any similarity relation, however,
but on the only common hexachordal superset, 6-Z25, which, as noted
above, is a subset of the basic harmony, 7–32.[68]

With the new entrance of the chromatic motive, beginning on G#, the
harmony changes to 6-Z43,[69] a set that occurred in the previous section
(Ex. 92). Although 6-Z43 is somewhat remote from the main harmonic
sets, its connection to 6-Z19, which follows, is clear in the context: They
share a common subset type, 5–20. (That is, they are maximally similar
with respect to pc; however, the relation is not explicitly represented by
the two forms in this instance.)

The change from 6-Z19 to 6–27 (Ex. 94) represents the maximal change
possible with respect to interval content between two hexachords (6-Z19:
[313431]; 6–27: [225222]). At the same time, the two sets share a 5-
note subset type: 5–16, one of the main harmonies in the work. Again,
however, the latter relation is not explicitly represented in this context,
and the dissimilar interval-content feature predominates.

68. Since 6-Z25 is a subset of both 7–35 and 7–32 it affords a specific link between
the diatonic and atonal components here, the juxtaposition of which characterizes
much of the music of the work, as has been observed frequently above.

69. In the duet score there is no change of harmony here; 5–20 continues until the
following measure. This is peculiar because the sketch (short score) of the passage on
Sketchbook p. 92 clearly changes to 6-Z43 as in the full score.

Ex. 95. *Sacrificial Dance:* R157

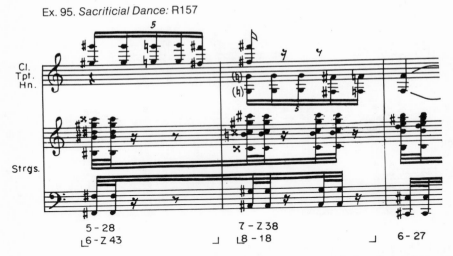

Example 95 shows the subsequent development of the chromatic motive and accompanying harmonies. Whereas the combination of the motive and the chord at R155+1 (Ex. 94) produces a relatively inconsequential set (with reference to *The Rite of Spring*), namely, 8–2, at R157f, it forms the significant sets bracketed in Ex. 95: 6–Z43 and 8–18. The reference to the latter fundamental harmony is unequivocal here; both 6–Z43 (and 6–Z17) and 6–27 are related to it by inclusion. In connection with the occurrence of 6–27 here it is important to observe that the last note of the chromatic motive, F, is an integral element of the set. Unlike previous endings of the motive, all sixteenth-note values, this one is held through two measures.

Ex. 96. *Sacrificial Dance:* R158

At R158 is the next-to-last occurrence of the chromatic motive in the form that begins on G# (Ex. 96). Both harmonies are forms of 7–19, the second a transposition ($t = 11$) of the first. Set 7–19 is one of the 7-note subsets of 8–18 (along with the more familiar 7-note sets, 7–16, 7–31, and 7–32). Its role here appears to be that of surrogate for 8–18. Neither 7–19 nor its complement is prominent elsewhere in the work (cf. Exx. 63c, 66a, 66c). Set 6–27 at the end of Ex. 96, is, of course, identical to 6–27 at the end of Ex. 95.

At R159, set 6–Z19 returns in the form shown in Ex. 94 and is repeated until R161 (exactly 19 metrical pulses! cf. n. 67), where it serves as point of departure for the climactic progression. This progression is identical to the one shown in Ex. 56a, from Sketchbook p. 104, discussed in connection with *Introduction to Part 2*. The corresponding sketch for this passage in *Sacrificial Dance* occurs on Sketchbook p. 85 and is in red ink with appended staves drawn in containing a correction in the orthography of the first two chords. From this change in orthography, carried over to the sketch on p. 104, it is clear that the passage was originally conceived for the *Sacrificial Dance* and then transferred to the *Introduction to Part 2*, where it underwent elaboration as discussed above in connection with R82–R83. Stravinsky's predilection for this progression very likely is based on the fact that it contains many, if not all, of the basic harmonies of the work.

From R162 through R164+2 there is a modified return of the music that was initially stated at R149. The major modification here results from transposition, with $t = 10$, one of four values of t that produce maximum invariance. There are, incidentally, exactly 17 metrical pulses (including rests) from R162 to the introduction of the chromatic motive at R163, another of the instances of prime number mentioned above (n. 67). This return to the music at R149 evidently was not part of the original plan of the movement. On Sketchbook p. 95, the last page of the short score for this section, the special passage that ends at R161+1 is followed immediately by the music at R165 in the final version.[70]

The ending of the section, shown in Ex. 97, involves three sonorities (excluding the turn figure on the upper staff). Of these 6–Z43 is familiar from the music immediately preceding; the form in Ex. 97 is a transposition of the form shown in Ex. 95, with $t = 6$. Set 7–31 is, of course, one

70. For graphic reasons this reading of the continuity of the sketches is somewhat problematic, however. The first sketch is in short score layout and in both light and heavy pencil. The second sketch is in light pencil with horn parts indicated in black ink and the layout is reduced to three staves with a few indications of instrumentation inserted. There are no sketches for the missing passage (R162–R164+2).

Ex. 97. *Sacrificial Dance:* R166+2

of the basic harmonies,[71] and, remarkably, here at the end of the section set 6-Z49 is the complement of the opening set of the movement, 6-Z28 (Ex. 88a). Indeed, 6-Z28 follows immediately at the beginning of the next section, which is a transposition of the opening section of the movement. The transposition is such that 6-Z28 is the literal complement of 6-Z49:[72] 6-Z49 in Ex. 97 is [3,4,6,7,10,0] and 6-Z28 at R167 is [8,9,11,1,2,5]. Just as 6-Z49 is a subset of 7–31 and contains 5–32, so 6-Z28 is a subset of 7–32 and contains 5–31. Once again, the families of two of the 7-note sets are linked in a very specific way by the two hexachords in this local context.

R167–R173+2

As remarked above, this section is a transposition of the opening section, from R142 up to R149. The particular transposition ($t = 11$) appears to have no special significance.[73]

R174–R180

The ostinato figure that underlies the entire section first appears in full on Sketchbook p. 96 (Ex. 98) in green ink, although there are some hints at the configuration on p. 83 bottom and p. 84 bottom.

Ex. 98. Sketchbook p. 96

5-7

The set is 5–7, which has not been prominent heretofore.[74] Although it

71. The harmony is 6-27 in the piano duet.

72. In the full score at R166+4 trombone 2 has a B. There is little doubt that this should be corrected to Bb, however, since it seems clear that the trombones double horns at the unison. If B is correct, the sonority reduces to set 7-22 (see Ex. 49a).

73. The choice of particular pitch levels is especially interesting and elusive when one compares Sketchbook entries with final versions. Stravinsky's note at the bottom of Sketchbook p. 87 reminding him to transpose the section to C# major does not, of course, imply a traditional tonal orientation but is merely the only way he would have had to express the transpositional relation. From this note, which specifies a continuation beginning with the ostinato figure at R174, one might assume that the transposition effected some kind of pitch continuity with the forthcoming new section. This is not substantiated, however.

74. In many recorded performances, even recent ones by eminent conductors, the beginning of the section is treated as though it featured the percussion section, timpani in particular, and it is virtually impossible to hear the ostinato figure. There is no indication in the score to justify this interpretation.

does not derive from 6-Z43, the final harmony at the end of the preceding section, it does relate to the complement of 6-Z43 (6-Z17) because it is a subset of the latter. Of the fundamental harmonies in *The Rite of Spring* overall, however, set 5-7 relates most importantly to 4–16 and its complement. This relation is made explicit with the entrance of the whole-tone theme (4–21) at R175+1 (Ex. 99a), which creates, with the ostinato figure, the large set 8–16. Moreover, just as the theme ends, on F# at R176, the tetrachord 4–16 is stated as shown in Ex. 99b.

Ex. 99a. *Sacrificial Dance:* R175+1

Ex. 99b. *Sacrificial Dance:* R176

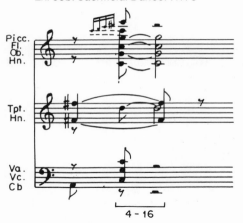

This section contains two thematic components that do not fit well into the overall harmonic scheme and that are to be accounted for mainly as local events. The first of these is shown in Ex. 100a.

Ex. 100a. *Sacrificial Dance:* R176+1

The upper parts here imitate the contour of the whole-tone theme in Ex. 99a and serve as counterpoint to the augmentation of 4–21 in the lower parts. Nevertheless, the sets formed by the individual lines are not significant. Only when the total configuration is taken into account is there a connection to the main harmonies of the work, for 7–25 contains 6–27 (cf. Exx. 32, 66a).

The melodic configuration at R177 is less anomalous but still problematic, owing to a large extent to the complicated orchestration, which is made even more complicated in the ill-conceived recorded performances to which one has access. (The problem is one of orchestral balance and voicing.)

Ex. 100b. *Sacrificial Dance:* R177

As shown in Ex. 100b, the principal melodic thread here is based on set 6–8, which relates to the family of diatonic sets through its subset 5–23. The latter is formed by contiguous pitches, as indicated in Ex. 100b.

Ex. 101. *Sacrificial Dance:* R180

The section ends on the tutti chord shown in Ex. 101, the fundamental harmony 5–32.[75] This is followed immediately by 6-Z42, which initiates the brief (6 measure) return of the first section of the movement.

75. In the 1943 revision Stravinsky changed this chord to 7–31, a remarkable substitution, since both harmonies are so basic to *The Rite of Spring.*

R181–R185+3

The ostinato figure (Ex. 98) is resumed in this section. However, the music here is far more complex than in the section from R174 to R180, where the ostinato figure was first introduced. Indeed, this is one of the most intricate sections in *The Rite of Spring,* and a reading of the harmonies is correspondingly difficult. The ostinato figure (Ex. 98) and the whole-tone theme (Ex. 99a) remain in the forefront, but additional components create a very thick and active texture. These consist of a succession of triads introduced by clarinets after R181, the secondary theme (Ex. 100b) brought in by trumpets at R181+2, and a transposed replica of the ostinato figure played in the upper register by Eb clarinet and D trumpet beginning at R184, as the theme is transposed to begin on G.

Ex. 102. Sketchbook p. 85

The triadic component together with the whole-tone theme was evidently conceived as a separate level, judging from the first sketch of the passage on Sketchbook p. 85 reproduced in Ex. 102. The succession of triads taken by itself exhibits a certain degree of regularity: Each pair forms 6-Z19 whenever the transposition is 1 or 11 (e.g., the first pair in Ex. 102); whenever the transposition is 2 or 10 the diatonic set 6–33 is formed. However, the vertical dimension over the entire texture is not highly regulated: Several harmonies are formed that do not relate to the basic structures of the work and that do not occur elsewhere in the music. The more familiar ones include 8-Z15, 5–16, 5–32, 6-Z13/42, 6–27, 6-Z43, and 6-Z49.

R186–R201+3

At R186 set 6–30 closes the previous section and serves as point of departure for the new section, a modified repetition of part of the first section
of the movement that begins here with 6-Z42, as at R146. When the bass
note C is added, the sonority becomes the fundamental harmony 7–16, as
indicated in Ex. 103 (cf. Ex. 91).[76]

Ex. 103. *Sacrificial Dance:* R186

With respect to this initial statement at R146, transposition is the main
modification here, with $t = 7$; the transposition has no unusual effect.
From R186 through R189+1 the reiterated sets are those of the corresponding passages at the beginning of the movement: 6–27, 6-Z42, and
7–16; because both hexachords are subsets of 7–16, the entire passage
(R186–R189+1) is controlled by the latter. Although this section appears
to be merely a transposition of the material in the earlier section, there
are some significant differences. These will be pointed out in the following
discussion.

    R189+2 brings a return to the progression at R144 (Ex. 90), but here
the third chord is different. Whereas it is 6-Z19 in the previous passage(s),
here it is 7–32. On Sketchbook p. 88, the chord is 6-Z19, which means,
clearly, that Stravinsky made a change at the time the duet score was completed. The change is significant insofar as it substantiates the extent to
which Stravinsky worked out his sonorities within a specific scheme, for
6-Z19 is a subset of 7–32, it will be recalled. Similarly, at the same place
in the Sketchbook (p. 88) the last chord in the measure is 6-Z19, not the
subset of 6-Z19 (5–20), as in the final version.

76. In the duet score pc1 is missing. As a consequence the set is (incorrectly) 6-Z39.

Ex. 104. *Sacrificial Dance:* R192

The set 7–16, which follows (R189+2) immediately (as in Ex. 103), is in marked contrast to it, for it contains none of the sets in that measure. This juxtaposition of 7–16 and 7–32 is intensified at R192, as shown in Ex. 104, where the gigantic sonorities reduce to the sets named below the bottom staff in that example (Ex. 104). Indeed, as is evident, this passage contains not only 7–16 and 7–32 but also 5–31 and five hexachords. A set-complex interpretation of the relations among all these components reveals that 5–31 is in K or Kh to all the hexachords except 6-Z43, which is neither in the relation K nor Kh to any of the 5- or 7-element sets here. Set 6–27 is the only set that relates (Kh) to 7–16, 5–31, and 7–32 and hence is the nexus hexachord for the passage. Set 5–31 connects all the hexachords except 6-Z43, as remarked above.

The precursor of this passage in the first section, shown in Ex. 92, shares only one harmony with it, 6-Z43. There 6-Z43 is in the relation K to the two 5-element sets, 5–20 and 5–22. Thus, its occurrence here at R192 may perhaps be explained in terms of its role in the earlier passage.

Ex. 105. *Sacrificial Dance:* R193+4

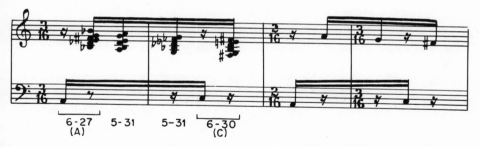

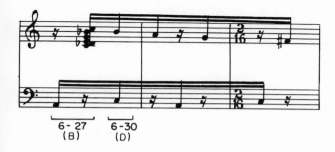

In the passage that follows that shown in Ex. 104 set 5-31 remains the predominant harmony. The two hexachords there (Ex. 105)[77] are in the relation Kh to 5-31. Moreover, the two forms of 6-27 (marked A and B in Ex. 105) are transpositionally related, with $t = 3$, yielding a common 5-note subset of type 5-31. The two occurrences of 6-30 (C and D) are identical with respect to pitch-class content. More interesting is the fact that the D replaces the A form of 6-27 as harmonization of the upper-voice Bb. The invariant subset between the two is again 5-31 [10,1,4,6,7]. One additional aspect of Ex. 105 needs to be mentioned. The upper voice melody undergoes what has often been called an additive process here: A-G-F# becomes Bb-A-G-F-# and then C-Bb-A-G-F#. The latter 5-note group is nontrivial in terms of *The Rite of Spring*, for the set formed is 5-10 (cf. Exx. 53, 77). Its ordering here producing alternate whole and half steps points up its relation to the octatonic scale, set 8-28.[78]

Example 106 shows the concluding passage of *The Rite of Spring*. In some ways this is among the more perplexing passages in the work. Specifically, it is almost impossible to decide what the main upper voice is intended to be. In the piano duet version the upper voice at R201 is G-C-E-F, a continuation of the previous pattern. Yet in the full score the separate beaming of the uppermost *divisi* section of the first violins indicates that the upper voice is G-C-E-C. This motion is then completed with F# in the next measure, forming set 4-Z29, a familiar set in *The Rite of Spring*. However this may be, clearly the most important feature consists of the verticals shown in Ex. 106.

The first vertical is 6-Z29, a set that has occurred before (e.g., Ex. 90). This chord together with the bass A forms 7-32, as before. The same pc form of 7-32 returns again on the fourth 16th note of the measure, following 6-Z43, another familiar set in the *Sacrificial Dance*. The chord preceding the climactic first chord in R201+1 is 6-33. Although this set belongs primarily to the diatonic sphere, it does relate directly to two of the sets that are important in this closing passage, 4-Z29 and, more significantly, the final chord, 4-16 (cf. Exx. 67a, 67b).

77. In order to represent this passage in condensed form on two staves it was necessary to make certain enharmonic adjustments with respect to the full score.

78. The horns in the passage shown in Ex. 105 have sets of the same type: 4-27. To extract this subset and endow it with particular significance would be fallacious, however. What is involved here is not harmony but instrumental voicing. This is clear from the piano duet. However, 4-27 and its complement are important sets elsewhere in the music.

Ex. 106. *Sacrificial Dance:* R201

The climactic chord in R201+1 is 8–18, as shown in Ex. 106.[79] Only two other instances of this large set have been discussed (**Exx.** 1, 56a); however, there are multiple occurrences of its complement, 4–18 (**Exx.** 2, 3, 4, 5, 31, 40, 42, 44, 56a, 65, 66, 71, 74, 83c, 88b). Indeed, it seems that this is the most frequently encountered tetrachord in the entire work, and a final reference to it through its complement is appropriate here.

The 9-note group following the climactic statement of 8–18 does not form a significant set but is gestural (notated as a glissando in the duet). The same is evidently true for all of R201+2, for the set formed there is 4–6, a new set in the work, and it is unlikely that Stravinsky would introduce new harmonies at this final moment in the work.

The final chord is 4–16. Again, this choice is based on previous occur-rences of the set. For instance, it has served a cadential or articulative function previously (**Exx.** 9, 99b), and it is a prominent set in the *Intro-duction to Part 2,* in particular as the ostinato figure shown in Ex. 10.

The ending of *The Rite of Spring* caused Stravinsky some difficulty. In connection with Ex. 87 it has already been pointed out that the *Ritual of the Ancestors* was originally intended to be the final movement and to follow the *Sacrificial Dance.* When we examine that closing passage (Ex. 87) and its relation to the final version of the ending of the *Sacrificial Dance,* it is astonishing to recognize that the final chord of the latter, 4–16, is the complement of the final configuration in Ex. 87 (8–16).

Ex. 107. Sketchbook p. 87

More germane to the final version of the ending of the *Sacrificial Dance* are the sketches on pp. 87–89 of the *Rite of Spring* Sketchbook. In a pen-cil sketch on p. 87 (Ex. 107)—the only pencil sketch on the page—appear two chords. The first of these, 7–32, is identical in pc content (not ver-tical arrangement) to the forms of 7–32 shown in Ex. 106; the second is almost identical in pc content to 8–18 as shown in Ex. 106. The set, how-

79. It is possible that the set is 7–19 in the full score, as it is in the piano duet, since only the alto flute has concert A, whereas all the other pitches are played by at least two instruments.

ever, is 7–31 [4,6,7,9,10,1]. This is evidently an abstract sketch for sonorities in the version of the ending sketched in ink in an adjacent position on the same sketch page (87). This ink sketch is the original ending of the work (excluding the premature ending shown in Ex. 87, which involved another movement, *Ritual of the Ancestors*). The verticals are those shown in the first part of Ex. 104 except that the first chord, including the bass, is 6-Z19 [9,10,0,1,4,5]. That is, a subset of 7–32, the first chord shown in Ex. 107, is used in place of the 7–32 shown in Ex. 104. Set 7–31, as in the pencil sketch (Ex. 107), is used as the climactic chord in the ink sketch in place of 8–18 in the final version.[80] Once again, we note the association of 7–32 and 7–31. This is followed by the trill and the glissando and then by the figure shown in Ex. 108.

Ex. 108. Sketchbook p. 87

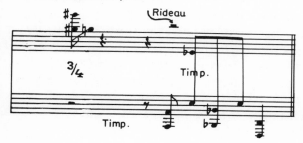

This is the timpani figure introduced at R174 based upon 5–7 (Ex. 98) but transposed and truncated. The set formed is 4–8, which is of relatively minor importance in *The Rite of Spring,* but taking into account the transposition ($t = 5$), it is apparent that the G# in the upper part is the note required to complete the set 5–7. At first this ending, the statement of 5–7 in particular, seems very different from the final version. Further investigation, however, reveals that 4–16, the closing set of the final version, is a subset of 5–7. In Ex. 108, 4–16 is represented by the pitches G#, Eb, Bb, and D.

In the Sketchbook at the top of p. 88 is still another version of the passage that leads to the ending. This is obviously a development of the music preceding the original ending and discussed in connection with Ex. 108. Here the climactic chord, which occurs simultaneously with the string tremolo, is 6–30, not 8–18 as in the final version or 7–31 as in the original ending.

80. Typical of Stravinsky, the lower part of the chord is spelled Gb-Bb-Db-Gb, whereas in the pencil sketch the same part is spelled F#-Bb-C#-F# (Ex. 107).

On Sketchbook p. 89 is a full-score layout of the climactic chord with the string tremolo, followed by the ascending glissando, here culminating in the dyad G-G#. There follows a note to the effect that the ending is on the preceding page, i.e., the original ending in short score discussed above in connection with Ex. 108. Here in this fully orchestrated version, the climactic chord remains 6-30. From these differences it can be concluded that the composer ultimately chose to use the largest set of the family of sets to which 7-31, 6-30, and 8-18 belong—another and final testament to his consistent and logical choice of harmonies in *The Rite of Spring*.[81]

Summary of Harmonic Relations

Because of the large number of harmonies involved in *The Rite of Spring*, it is essential to select the main harmonies with care and with a cetain degree of flexibility. A set-complex chart that includes virtually all the sets is useful but requires thoughtful interpretation. One should take into account not only the number of set-complex relations (both K and Kh) of a set but also the number of times the set occurs and its mode of occurrence. For example, set 5-25 has many set-complex relations, yet it is a set of relatively minor importance in the music. On the basis of the previous chronological survey of the various movements of *The Rite of Spring*, certain sets are very prominent. Of these, three 7-note sets (7-16, 7-31, and 7-32) and four 8-note sets (8-16, 8-18, 8-28, and 8-23) have been selected as main harmonies.

Before considering the set-complex relations for the sets listed above, it should be pointed out that the following inclusions hold:

> 7-16 contains 5-32, 5-31 and 5-16;
> 7-31 contains 5-32, 5-16, and 5-31; and
> 7-32 contains 5-31, 5-16, and 5-32.

That is, each of the 7-note sets contains its own complement as well as the complement of the other two (at least once.)[82] Moreover, for the 8-note sets, we have the following inclusions:

---

81. These sets have interacted before (see, e.g., Ex. 21a).

82. The number of times the subset is represented in the main set is enclosed in parentheses in the following list. 7-16: 5-16 (1), 5-31 (3) 5-32 (1); 7-31: 5-31 (3), 5-16 (3), 5-32 (3); and 7-32: 5-32 (1), 5-16 (1), 5-31 (3). It is interesting that in each case 5-31 is maximally represented.

8-28 contains 4-28 and 4-18;

8-23 contains 4-23, 4-18 and 4-16;

8-18 contains 4-28, 4-23, 4-18, and 4-16; and

8-16 contains 4-23, 4-18 and 4-16.

The mutual inclusions that form such a complete pattern in the case of the 7-note sets do not hold here; only 8-18 contains all the 4-note complements.

Examples 109–30 present tables of set complexes and set complexes derived by set-theoretic operations on two or more set complexes. Excluded from these tables are sets that do not occur in *The Rite of Spring*. In a remarkable number of cases, however, the subsets or supersets are represented exhaustively in the music. Such cases are indicated by a note on the example.

Examples 109–11 require minimal comments. Example 109, the list of sets that comprise the set complex K about 7-16, may serve as model for the others. (The sign # designates cardinal number of the sets listed below.) In the case of the Z-related hexachords the main set never contains both members. The parentheses indicate which one is not contained in the main set. In all the lists (Exx. 109–30) it is never necessary to give more than two columns representing sets of two cardinal numbers, because each cardinal number stands for its inverse as well. The asterisk designates which of the larger sets is a superset of the main set in the set complex as indicated in the note below Ex. 109.

As indicated in the notes below Examples 109–11, all the 8-note supersets of the three main sets occur in the music. Indeed, they are among the more significant of the large sets throughout the work. Recall, for instance, 8-27 together with 4-27 in the passage shown in Ex. 60. Even more astounding is the fact that all the hexachords of 7-31 and 7-32 are components of the music. Thus, it is not merely the large roster of sets in the union of the three that indicates their importance over the entire work but also the exhaustive occurrence of their 6-note subsets and 8-note supersets.

Examples 112–14 display the intersection of set complexes formed by pairs of set complexes. In the absence of a specific contextual guide, it is not possible to say that the relation to one set or the other is more important; the abstract connection to both sets is part of the general harmonic scheme. Consider, for example, the complement-related pair 6-Z13 and 6-Z42. Set 6-Z42 is a subset of 7-16, while its complement is a subset of 7-31. Thus, this set pair links the two different sets, in the abstract. In some cases there may be a more specific statement, however, as in Ex.

Example 109
K(7–16)

#6	#4	
3/(36)	2	13
(13)/42	3*	Z15
15	4	17*
(19)/44	5	18*
27	7	19
28/(49)	8	26
(10)/39	10	27
	11	28
	12*	Z29*

All the hexachords of 7–16 occur in *The Rite of Spring*. All 8-note supersets of 7–16 occur in *The Rite of Spring*.

*The 8-note complement is a superset of the nexus set, 7–16.

Example 110
K(7–31)

#6	#4	
13/(42)	3	18*
23/(45)	9	25
27	10	26
(28)/49	12*	27*
(29)/50	13*	28*
30	Z15	Z29
	17	

All the hexachords of 7–31 occur in *The Rite of Spring*. All 8-note supersets of 7–31 occur in *The Rite of Spring*.

*The 8-note complement is a superset of the nexus set, 7–31.

Example 111
K(7–32)

#6	#4	
19/(44)	3	16
24/(46)	7	17*
25/(47)	8	18*
27	10	19
28/(49)	11	23
29/(50)	12	26*
31	13	27*
	14	28
	Z15*	Z29

All the hexachords of 7–32 occur in *The Rite of Spring*. All 8-note supersets of 7–32 occur in *The Rite of Spring*.

*The 8-note complement is a superset of the nexus set, 7–32.

Example 112
·[K(7–16), K(7–31)]

#6	#4	
13/42	3	18
27	10	26
28/49	12	27
	13	28
	Z15	Z29
	17	

Example 113
·[K(7–16, K(7–32)]

#6	#4	
19/44	3	17
27	7	18
28/(49)	8	19
	10	26
	11	27
	12	28
	13	Z29
	Z15	

Example 114
·[K(7–31, K(7–32)]

#6	#4	
27	3	18
28/49	10	26
29/50	12	27
	13	28
	Z15	Z29
	17	

Example 115
·[K(7–16), K(7–31), K(7–32)]

#6	#4[†]	
27	3	18
28/49	10	26
	12	27
	13	28
	Z15	Z29
	17	

[†]This set of sets corresponds exactly to that in ·[K(7–16), K(7–31)].

104, where 6-Z42 is explicitly given as a subset of 7-16 by the segmentation of the music at that point.

Perhaps the most interesting of the intersecting set complexes is that shown in Ex. 115: the intersection of all three set complexes. This includes the hexachord 6-27, so fundamental to *The Rite of Spring,* as well as the less significant pair 6-Z28 and 6-Z49. It is surprising that this set complex corresponds almost completely to the intersection of K(7-16) and K(7-31). And, of course, this set complex is a subset of the intersection of the set complexes of any of the pairs.

Examples 116-19 show the results of the operation symmetric difference Δ (or exclusive union) on the set complexes about the three 7-note sets. The operation can be explained as follows: If A-B is the set of sets in A but not in B, then the symmetric difference of A and B, symbolized by Δ (A,B), is the union (set-theoretic sum) of A-B and B-A. Hence, symmetric difference is a measure of the belongedness of a set; a set in a particular example is a subset of only one of the sets named at the top of the example. Symmetric difference is therefore the converse of intersection, as can be seen by comparing Ex. 116 with Ex. 112, Ex. 117 with Ex. 113, and so on. The comparison of Δ sets with · sets[83] is interesting in a number of ways. In general, the sizes of the Δ sets are relatively large compared with the sizes of the · sets. In particular, the Δ sets include many more of the hexachords, thus pointing up the special associations that many of those hexachords have in the music. In this connection, special attention is drawn to Ex. 119. This is the complement of the set complex shown in Ex. 115, and comparison of the two will show, explicitly, which sets are links between at least two of the 7-note sets and which sets belong to only one of the 7-note sets.

Examples 120-25 display the set complexes K about four of the most prominent 8-note sets. Excluded from these lists, by definition of K and Kh, are the 4-note subsets. These relations were summarized above. Only 8-18, it will be recalled, contains all the complementary tetrachords. Moreover, sets 4-18 and 8-18 are perhaps the most important of the sets of those cardinalities, measured in terms of number of occurrences.

Certain comments about the set complexes of these 8-note sets are given below the examples. (Observe that here, as in the set complexes of the 7-note sets, the single asterisk indicates that the complement is also a subset of the nexus set, i.e., the relation Kh holds.) The comments on K(8-28), Ex. 122, are worth repeating here, since they are quite astonishing. All the 5-note subsets and 6-note subsets of 8-28 occur in *The Rite*

---

83. The symbol · signifies set-theoretic multiplication (intersection).

Example 116
Δ[K(7–16), K(7–31)]

#6	#4	
3/(36)	2	9
15	4	11
19/44	5	19
23/(45)	7	25
30	8	
(29)/50		

Example 117
Δ[K(7–16), K(7–32)]

#6	#4
3/(36)	2
(13)/42	4
15	5
24/(46)	14
25/(47)	16
29/(50)	23
31	

Example 118
Δ[K(7–31), K(7–32)]

#6	#4	
13/(42)	8	17
19/(44)	9	18
23/(45)	11	19
24/(46)	14	23
25/(47)	16	25
30		
31		

Example 119
Δ[K(7–16), K(7–31), K(7–32)]

#6	#4
3/(36)	2
15	4
23/(45)	5
30	9
24/(46)	14
25/(47)	16
31	23
	25

Example 120
K(8–16)

#6	#5	
5	6	22
6/38	7	23
17/43	9	25
(19)/44	11	26
(24)/46	Z12	27
25/47	14*	28
(29)/50	15*	32
31	Z18*	34
33	19	35
34	20*	Z36
	21	Z38

*The 7-note complement is also a subset of the nexus set, 8–16.

Example 121
K(8–18)

#6	#5†	
3/(36)	3	21
5	6	22*
13/42	7	23
15	10	25
17/43	Z12	26
19/44	14	27
23/(45)	15	28
24/(46)	16*	31*
25/(47)	Z17	32*
27	Z18*	Z36*
28/49	19*	Z38*
29/50	20	
31		

†All 7-note subsets of 8–18 occur in *The Rite of Spring*.

Example 122
K(8–28)

#6†	#5††
13/(42)	10
23/(45)	16
27	19
(28)/49	25
(29)/50	28
30	31**
	32

†All 6-note subsets of 8–28 occur in *The Rite of Spring*.
††All 5-note subsets of 8–28 occur in *The Rite of Spring*.
**All 7-note subsets of 8–28 reduce to a single set class: 7–31.

Example 123
K(8–23)

#6	#5	
(6)/38	7	25
8	9	27
(24)/46	11	32
25/47	Z12	34
(29)/50	14	35
32	19	Z36
33	20	Z38
	23	

Example 124
K(8–Z15)

#6	#5	
(3)/36	1	20
5	6	21
(6)/38	7	22
(13)/42	9	23
17/43	10	25
19/(44)	11	26
24/46	Z12	27
25/(47)	14	28
27	15	31
28/(49)	16	32
29/(50)	Z17	34
30	Z18	Z36
31	19	Z38
34		

Example 125
K(8–12)

#6	#5	
3/36	1	21
5	3	22
13/42	6	25
15	7	26
17/(43)	9	27
(19)/44	10	28
23/45	11	31
(24)/46	Z12	32
27	16	34
28/49	Z18	Z36
(29)/50	19	Z38
30		
31		
34		

of Spring. The same holds for the 7-note subsets, trivially, because any selection of 7 notes from 8-28 is reducible to a set type 7-31.

The relatively small size of K(8-28), Ex. 122, reflects the general situation with respect to that set complex: The complex is the smallest of all. Similarly, the large size of K(8-Z15) in Ex. 124 is not surprising, for it is one of the largest complexes of that cardinality.

The set complex about 8-23, the master diatonic set, is interesting because it contains a number of the sets that occur in a predominantly atonal context in *The Rite of Spring,* notably the characteristic and frequently occurring set, 5-32.

Examples 126–40 present the intersecting set complexes for the six 8-note sets under discussion: 8-12, 8-Z15, 8-16, 8-18, 8-23, and 8-28. Comments will be made only on the more interesting of these set complexes and will include mention of similarity relations. The latter are summarized in Ex. 142.

Example 126 lists the members of the intersecting set complex formed by 8-16 and 8-18. This is relatively large, with a total of 25 members. In general, the larger intersecting set complexes correspond to a significant similarity relation, usually R1 or R2. In this case, however, the relation is Rp (pitch-class similarity only).

Example 127, the intersecting set complex for 8-16 and 8-28, is the smallest of all, with only 3 members. Musically, this means that there is minimal association of the two sets.

In Ex. 129 we find that the list of 5-element members is the same as the list of 5-element members of K(8-23). That is, the intersection is complete with respect to elements of that cardinality in 8-23—total absorption. This may suggest that 8-16 and 8-23 are highly similar, but in fact they are maximally dissimilar with respect to interval content (R0) and maximally similar only with respect to pitch-class content (Rp) (see Ex. 142).

Comparison of Ex. 131 with Ex. 127 reveals that they are almost identical; the former, the set complex about 8-23 and 8-28, contains one more member. Thus, 8-16 is minimally associated with 8-28, and 8-23 is minimally associated with 8-28. Nevertheless, 8-16 and 8-23 intersect in a number of sets (Ex. 129).

The intersecting set complex shown in Ex. 132, for 8-Z15 and 8-28 resembles that shown in Ex. 128, for 8-18 and 8-28. Set 8-Z15, however, is maximally dissimilar to 8-28 (R0). Also, it should be observed that all the 5-note subsets of 8-28 are included in the list in Ex. 132.

The intersecting set complex for 8-Z15 and 8-18 shown in Ex. 134 is

Example 126
·[K(8–16), K(8–18)]

#6	#5	
5	6	22
17/43	7	23
19/44	Z12	25
24/46	14	26
25/47	15	27
29/50	Z18	28
31	19	32
	20	Z36
	21	Z38

Example 127
·[K(8–16), K(8–28)]

#6	#5
(29)/50	19
	32

Example 128
·[K(8–18), K(8–28)]

#6	#5
13/42	10
23/(45)	16
27	19
28/49	25
29/50	31
	32

Example 129
·[K(8–16), K(8–23)]

#6	#5	
24/46	7	25
25/47	9	27
(29)/50	11	32
33	Z12	34
	14	35
	19	Z36
	20	Z38
	23	

one of the two largest such complexes under consideration here, but again the sets are related in divergent ways: the relation R0 and Rp holds. The association of these two sets, represented by their complements 4-Z15 and 4-18, is especially evident in *The Rite of Spring* (see, e.g., Exx. 3a, 3c, 31, 66a).

Example 135 again shows a large intersecting set complex, about 8-Z15 and 8-16. Only 6-33 and 5-35, both diatonic sets, are not included in the lists here.

The intersecting set complex for 8-12 and 8-16 is relatively large, and here the two sets are maximally similar with respect to interval content (R1) and with respect to pitch class (Rp). The same relations hold between 8-12 and 8-18 (Ex. 139) and their intersecting set complex is next to largest.

Example 140 shows the intersecting set complex for 8-12 and 8-Z15. This is the other of the two largest set complexes (cf. Ex. 134). Once again, the sets are maximally similar with respect to interval and pitch (R2 and Rp). Only the hexachordal pair 6-Z25/47 in 8-Z15 is excluded from the intersection.

Finally, Ex. 141 shows the intersection of all six 8-note sets paired off in the preceding examples. As might be expected, this is a very small set complex indeed. In fact, it is almost the same as the small set complex formed by the intersection of 8-16 and 8-28 (Ex. 127). Note, however, the important linkage provided by the fundamental set 5-32, so significant throughout the work. This small intersecting set complex can be interpreted as minimal harmonic association over the group of six fundamental sets that have been discussed here. Perhaps this provides some measure of the complexity of the work. I hope that at least it elucidates the complicated connection of components to some extent.

The lists presented in Exx. 109–41 spell out in precise detail relations among the pitch structures in *The Rite of Spring*. A more concise display of important relations is given in Ex. 143, which shows some of the main hexachords in the work and their principal subsets and supersets. In this list the Z-related hexachords are given together. As one result of this pairing, the subset-superset exchange is pointed up. Observe, for example, the pair 6-Z28 and 6-Z49. Pc set 6-Z28 has subset 5-31 while 6-Z49 has 7-31. The exchange holds between 5-16 and 5-32 and their complements as well.

Example 130
·[K(8–18), K(8–23)]

#6	#5	
24/46	7	25
25/47	Z12	27
29/50	14	32
	19	Z36
	20	Z38
	23	

Example 131
·[K(8–23), K(8–28)]

#6	#5
29/50	19
	25
	32

Example 132
·[K(8–Z15), K(8–28)]

#6	#5
13/42	10
27	16
30	19
28/49	25
29/50	31
	32

Example 133
·[K(8–Z15), K(8–23)]

#6	#5	
(6)/38	7	23
24/46	9	27
25/47	11	32
29/50	Z12	34
	14	Z36
	19	Z38
	20	

Example 134
·[K(8–Z15), K(8–18)]

#6	#5	
3/36	6	21
5	7	22
13/42	10	23
17/43	Z12	25
19/44	14	26
24/46	15	27
25/(47)	16	28
27	Z17	31
28/49	Z18	32
29/50	19	Z36
31	20	Z38

Example 135
·[K(8–Z15), K(8–16)]

#6	#5	
5	6	21
6/38	7	22
17/43	9	23
19/44	11	25
24/46	Z12	26
25/47	14	27
29/50	15	28
31	Z18	32
34	19	34
	20	Z36
		Z38

Example 136
·[K(8–12), K(8–28)]

#6	#5
13/42	10
23/45	16
27	19
28/49	25
29/50	28
30	31
	32

Example 137
·[K(8–12), K(8–23)]

#6	#5	
(24)/46	7	27
(29)/50	9	32
	11	34
	Z12	Z36
	19	Z38
	25	

Example 138
·[K(8–12), K(8–16)]

#6	#5	
5	6	25
17/43	7	26
(19)/44	9	27
(24)/46	11	28
(29)/50	Z12	32
31	Z18	34
34	19	Z36
	21	Z38
	22	

Example 139
·[K(8–12), K(8–18)]

#6	#5	
3/36	3	22
5	6	25
13/42	7	26
15	10	27
17/43	Z12	28
19/44	16	31
23/45	Z18	32
24/46	19	Z36
27	21	Z38
29/50		

Example 140
·[K(8–12), K(8–Z15)]

#6	#5	
3/36	1	22
5	6	25
13/42	7	26
17/43	9	27
19/44	10	28
24/46	11	31
27	Z12	32
28/49	16	34
29/50	Z18	Z36
30	19	Z38
31	21	
34		

Example 141
·[K(8–16), K(8–18), K(8–23), K(8–28), K(8–Z15), K(8–12)]

#6	#5
29/50	19
	25
	32

Example 142
Similarity Relations for Main Sets of Cardinal 4 (8)

12	12				
15	R2,Rp	15			
16	R1,Rp	R2,Rp	16		
18	R1,Rp	R0,Rp	Rp	18	
23	R0	Rp	R0,Rp	R0	23
28	Rp	R0	R0	Rp	

Example 143
Some of the Main Hexachords in *The Rite of Spring* with Principal
Subsets and Supersets

Hexachord	Subset	Superset
6–Z13	5–16	7–31
6–Z42	5–31	7–16
6–Z17	5–Z36	8–18
6–Z43	4–16	8–18
6–Z19	5–16	7–32
6–Z44	5–32	7–16
6–Z25	5–Z12	7–32
6–Z47	5–32	
6–27	5–16, 5–31, 5–32	7–16, 7–31, 7–32
6–Z28	5–31	7–16, 7–32
6–Z49	5–16, 5–32	7–31
6–Z29	5–31	7–32
6–Z50	5–32	7–31
6–30	5–31	7–31

Example 144
The Transitive Hexachordal Quintuple for the Relations R1 and Rp

	Examples
6–Z28	19, 51, 63b, 88a, 97
6–Z29	21, 47, 90, 106
6–30	21a, 24, 30, 33a, 49b, 55, 56a, 103, 104, 105
6–Z42	62, 77, 89, 103, 104
6–Z45	66a, 69, 70, 90, 104

As a final and, it is hoped, remarkable demonstration of the extent to which Stravinsky used very special relations in composing *The Rite of Spring*, Ex. 144 presents the transitive hexachordal quintuple for the relations R1 and Rp, along with a reference list of the examples in which these hexachords are cited in the present study. In each instance the common 5-note subset is 5–31! The hexachords, of course, are in the relation K to 7–31. Consequently, their complements are subsets of 7–31, although not supersets of 5–31.

Appendix

Prime Forms of the Pitch-Class Sets

Set name	Prime form	Set name	Prime form
3–1	0,1,2	9–1	0,1,2,3,4,5,6,7,8
3–2	0,1,3	9–2	0,1,2,3,4,5,6,7,9
3–3	0,1,4	9–3	0,1,2,3,4,5,6,8,9
3–4	0,1,5	9–4	0,1,2,3,4,5,7,8,9
3–5	0,1,6	9–5	0,1,2,3,4,6,7,8,9
3–6	0,2,4	9–6	0,1,2,3,4,5,6,8,10
3–7	0,2,5	9–7	0,1,2,3,4,5,7,8,10
3–8	0,2,6	9–8	0,1,2,3,4,6,7,8,10
3–9	0,2,7	9–9	0,1,2,3,5,6,7,8,10
3–10	0,3,6	9–10	0,1,2,3,4,6,7,9,10
3–11	0,3,7	9–11	0,1,2,3,5,6,7,9,10
3–12	0,4,8	9–12	0,1,2,4,5,6,8,9,10
4–1	0,1,2,3	8–1	0,1,2,3,4,5,6,7
4–2	0,1,2,4	8–2	0,1,2,3,4,5,6,8
4–3	0,1,3,4	8–3	0,1,2,3,4,5,6,9
4–4	0,1,2,5	8–4	0,1,2,3,4,5,7,8
4–5	0,1,2,6	8–5	0,1,2,3,4,6,7,8
4–6	0,1,2,7	8–6	0,1,2,3,5,6,7,8
4–7	0,1,4,5	8–7	0,1,2,3,4,5,8,9
4–8	0,1,5,6	8–8	0,1,2,3,4,7,8,9
4–9	0,1,6,7	8–9	0,1,2,3,6,7,8,9
4–10	0,2,3,5	8–10	0,2,3,4,5,6,7,9
4–11	0,1,3,5	8–11	0,1,2,3,4,5,7,9
4–12	0,2,3,6	8–12	0,1,3,4,5,6,7,9
4–13	0,1,3,6	8–13	0,1,2,3,4,6,7,9
4–14	0,2,3,7	8–14	0,1,2,4,5,6,7,9
4–Z15	0,1,4,6	8–Z15	0,1,2,3,4,6,8,9
4–16	0,1,5,7	8–16	0,1,2,3,5,7,8,9
4–17	0,3,4,7	8–17	0,1,3,4,5,6,8,9
4–18	0,1,4,7	8–18	0,1,2,3,5,6,8,9
4–19	0,1,4,8	8–19	0,1,2,4,5,6,8,9
4–20	0,1,5,8	8–20	0,1,2,4,5,7,8,9
4–21	0,2,4,6	8–21	0,1,2,3,4,6,8,10

Set name	Prime form	Set name	Prime form
4-22	0,2,4,7	8-22	0,1,2,3,5,6,8,10
4-23	0,2,5,7	8-23	0,1,2,3,5,7,8,10
4-24	0,2,4,8	8-24	0,1,2,4,5,6,8,10
4-25	0,2,6,8	8-25	0,1,2,4,6,7,8,10
4-26	0,3,5,8	8-26	0,1,2,4,5,7,9,10
4-27	0,2,5,8	8-27	0,1,2,4,5,7,8,10
4-28	0,3,6,9	8-28	0,1,3,4,6,7,9,10
4-Z29	0,1,3,7	8-Z29	0,1,2,3,5,6,7,9
5-1	0,1,2,3,4	7-1	0,1,2,3,4,5,6
5-2	0,1,2,3,5	7-2	0,1,2,3,4,5,7
5-3	0,1,2,4,5	7-3	0,1,2,3,4,5,8
5-4	0,1,2,3,6	7-4	0,1,2,3,4,6,7
5-5	0,1,2,3,7	7-5	0,1,2,3,5,6,7
5-6	0,1,2,5,6	7-6	0,1,2,3,4,7,8
5-7	0,1,2,6,7	7-7	0,1,2,3,6,7,8
5-8	0,2,3,4,6	7-8	0,2,3,4,5,6,8
5-9	0,1,2,4,6	7-9	0,1,2,3,4,6,8
5-10	0,1,3,4,6	7-10	0,1,2,3,4,6,9
5-11	0,2,3,4,7	7-11	0,1,3,4,5,6,8
5-Z12	0,1,3,5,6	7-Z12	0,1,2,3,4,7,9
5-13	0,1,2,4,8	7-13	0,1,2,4,5,6,8
5-14	0,1,2,5,7	7-14	0,1,2,3,5,7,8
5-15	0,1,2,6,8	7-15	0,1,2,4,6,7,8
5-16	0,1,3,4,7	7-16	0,1,2,3,5,6,9
5-Z17	0,1,3,4,8	7-Z17	0,1,2,4,5,6,9
5-Z18	0,1,4,5,7	7-Z18	0,1,2,3,5,8,9
5-19	0,1,3,6,7	7-19	0,1,2,3,6,7,9
5-20	0,1,3,7,8	7-20	0,1,2,4,7,8,9
5-21	0,1,4,5,8	7-21	0,1,2,4,5,8,9
5-22	0,1,4,7,8	7-22	0,1,2,5,6,8,9
5-23	0,2,3,5,7	7-23	0,2,3,4,5,7,9
5-24	0,1,3,5,7	7-24	0,1,2,3,5,7,9
5-25	0,2,3,5,8	7-25	0,2,3,4,6,7,9
5-26	0,2,4,5,8	7-26	0,1,3,4,5,7,9
5-27	0,1,3,5,8	7-27	0,1,2,4,5,7,9
5-28	0,2,3,6,8	7-28	0,1,3,5,6,7,9
5-29	0,1,3,6,8	7-29	0,1,2,4,6,7,9
5-30	0,1,4,6,8	7-30	0,1,2,4,6,8,9
5-31	0,1,3,6,9	7-31	0,1,3,4,6,7,9
5-32	0,1,4,6,9	7-32	0,1,3,4,6,8,9
5-33	0,2,4,6,8	7-33	0,1,2,4,6,8,10
5-34	0,2,4,6,9	7-34	0,1,3,4,6,8,10
5-35	0,2,4,7,9	7-35	0,1,3,5,6,8,10
5-Z36	0,1,2,4,7	7-Z36	0,1,2,3,5,6,8
5-Z37	0,3,4,5,8	7-Z37	0,1,3,4,5,7,8

Set name	Prime form	Set name	Prime form
5–Z38	0,1,2,5,8	7–Z38	0,1,2,4,5,7,8
6–1	0,1,2,3,4,5		
6–2	0,1,2,3,4,6		
6–Z3	0,1,2,3,5,6	6–Z36	0,1,2,3,4,7
6–Z4	0,1,2,4,5,6	6–Z37	0,1,2,3,4,8
6–5	0,1,2,3,6,7		
6–Z6	0,1,2,5,6,7	6–Z38	0,1,2,3,7,8
6–7	0,1,2,6,7,8		
6–8	0,2,3,4,5,7		
6–9	0,1,2,3,5,7		
6–Z10	0,1,3,4,5,7	6–Z39	0,2,3,4,5,8
6–Z11	0,1,2,4,5,7	6–Z40	0,1,2,3,5,8
6–Z12	0,1,2,4,6,7	6–Z41	0,1,2,3,6,8
6–Z13	0,1,3,4,6,7	6–Z42	0,1,2,3,6,9
6–14	0,1,3,4,5,8		
6–15	0,1,2,4,5,8		
6–16	0,1,4,5,6,8		
6–Z17	0,1,2,4,7,8	6–Z43	0,1,2,5,6,8
6–18	0,1,2,5,7,8		
6–Z19	0,1,3,4,7,8	6–Z44	0,1,2,5,6,9
6–20	0,1,4,5,8,9		
6–21	0,2,3,4,6,8		
6–22	0,1,2,4,6,8		
6–Z23	0,2,3,5,6,8	6–Z45	0,2,3,4,6,9
6–Z24	0,1,3,4,6,8	6–Z46	0,1,2,4,6,9
6–Z25	0,1,3,5,6,8	6–Z47	0,1,2,4,7,9
6–Z26	0,1,3,5,7,8	6–Z48	0,1,2,5,7,9
6–27	0,1,3,4,6,9		
6–Z28	0,1,3,4,7,9	6–Z49	0,1,3,5,6,9
6–Z29	0,1,3,6,8,9	6–Z50	0,1,4,6,7,9
6–30	0,1,3,6,7,9		
6–31	0,1,3,5,8,9		
6–32	0,2,4,5,7,9		
6–33	0,2,3,5,7,9		
6–34	0,1,3,5,7,9		
6–35	0,2,4,6,8,10